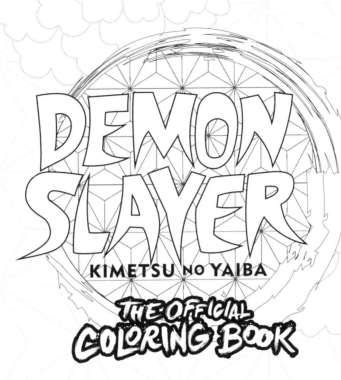

DEMON SLAYER

KIMETSU NO YAIBA

THE OFFICIAL COLORING BOOK

Art by

KOYOHARU GOTOUGE

KOYOHARU GOTOUGE

Hello! I'm Gotouge. I've put out a coloring book. I hope you enjoy it.

Ever since I was a child, I've never been very good at coloring, so I often found myself quitting halfway through. I also remember being shocked when I would see my friends' beautifully colored drawings. How about all of you?

Here are some tips:

+ Start with lighter colors and light shading.
+ Adjust the shade by layering the same color.
+ Do your best to color evenly.
+ Be careful to stay within the lines.

Above all, the key to coloring is believing in yourself and never giving up.

It might be fun to try coloring Tanjiro and his friends in different colors than usual. I will also give it a try with my Coupy-Pencils and colored pencils!

Wah—

**DEMON SLAYER: KIMETSU NO YAIBA
THE OFFICIAL COLORING BOOK**

Shonen Jump Edition

Art by
KOYOHARU GOTOUGE

KIMETSU NO YAIBA NURIE CHO - AO/AKA -
© 2021 by Koyoharu Gotouge
All rights reserved.
First published in Japan in 2021 by SHUEISHA Inc., Tokyo.
English translation rights arranged by SHUEISHA Inc.

DESIGN Jimmy Presler **SENIOR EDITOR** Amanda Ng

Printed in the U.S.A.

Published by VIZ Media, LLC
P.O. Box 77010
San Francisco, CA 94107

10 9 8 7 6 5 4 3 2 1
First printing, April 2022

ISBN: 978-1-9747-2911-1

viz.com

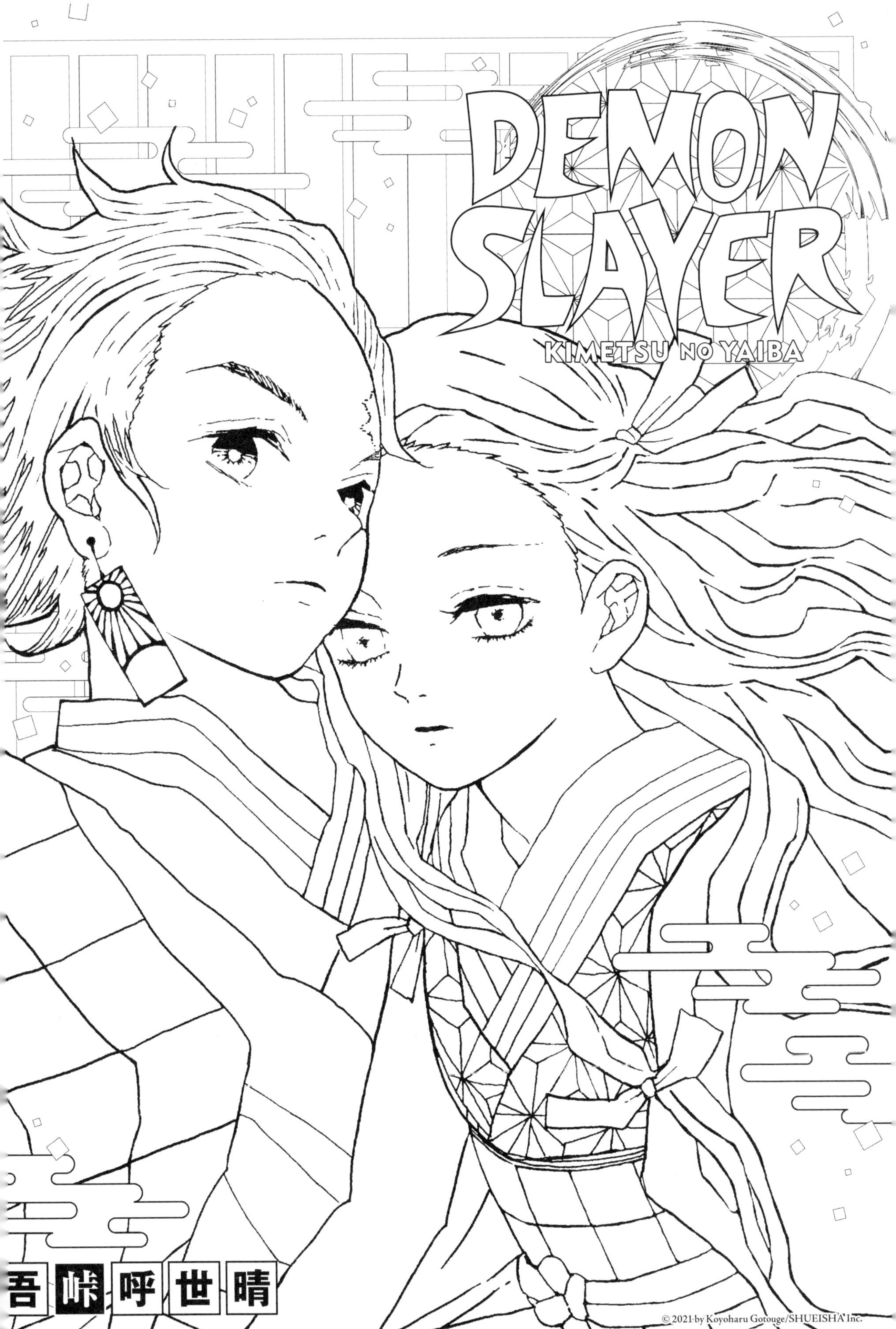
DEMON SLAYER
KIMETSU NO YAIBA
吾峠呼世晴

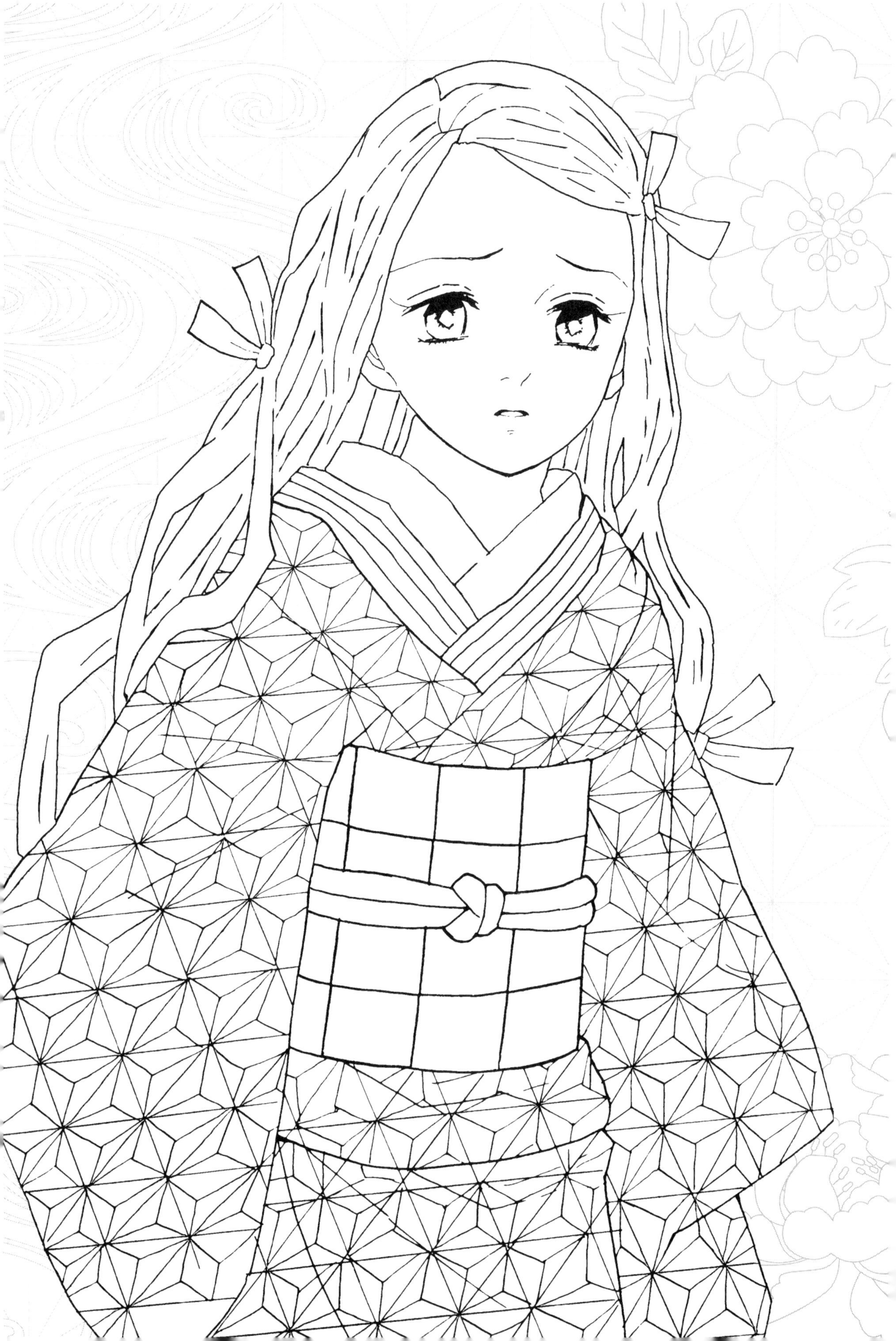

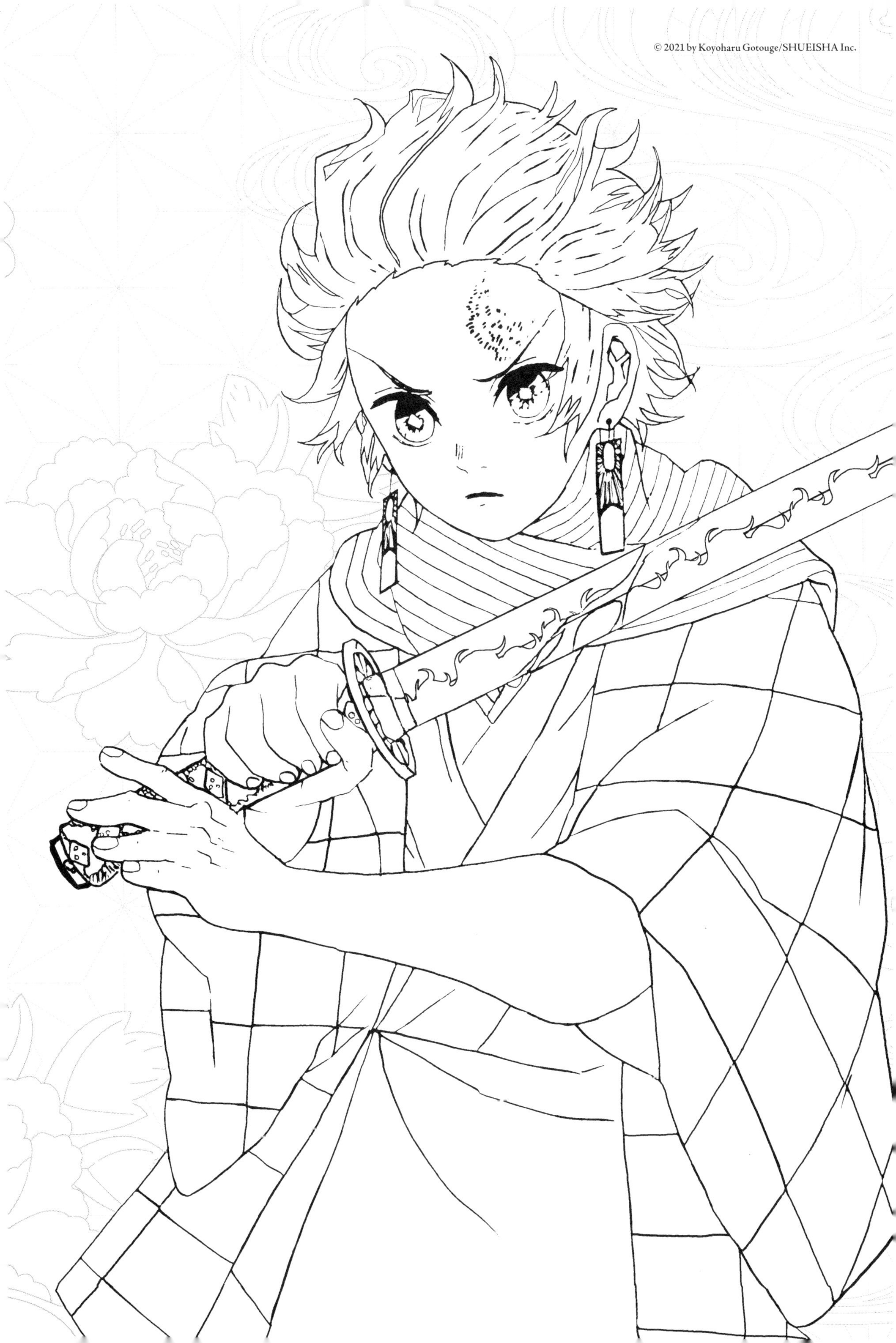

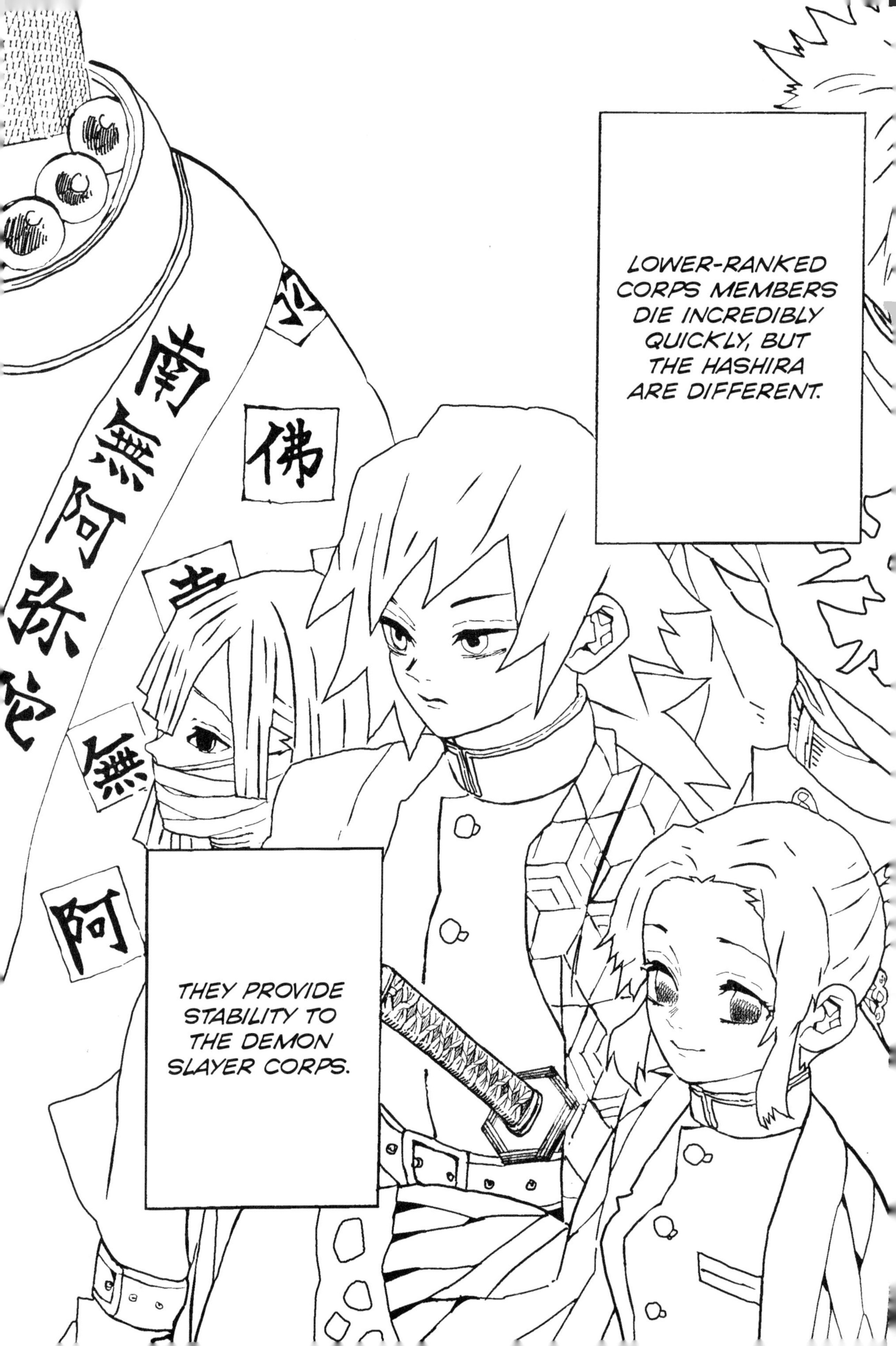
LOWER-RANKED CORPS MEMBERS DIE INCREDIBLY QUICKLY, BUT THE HASHIRA ARE DIFFERENT.
THEY PROVIDE STABILITY TO THE DEMON SLAYER CORPS.

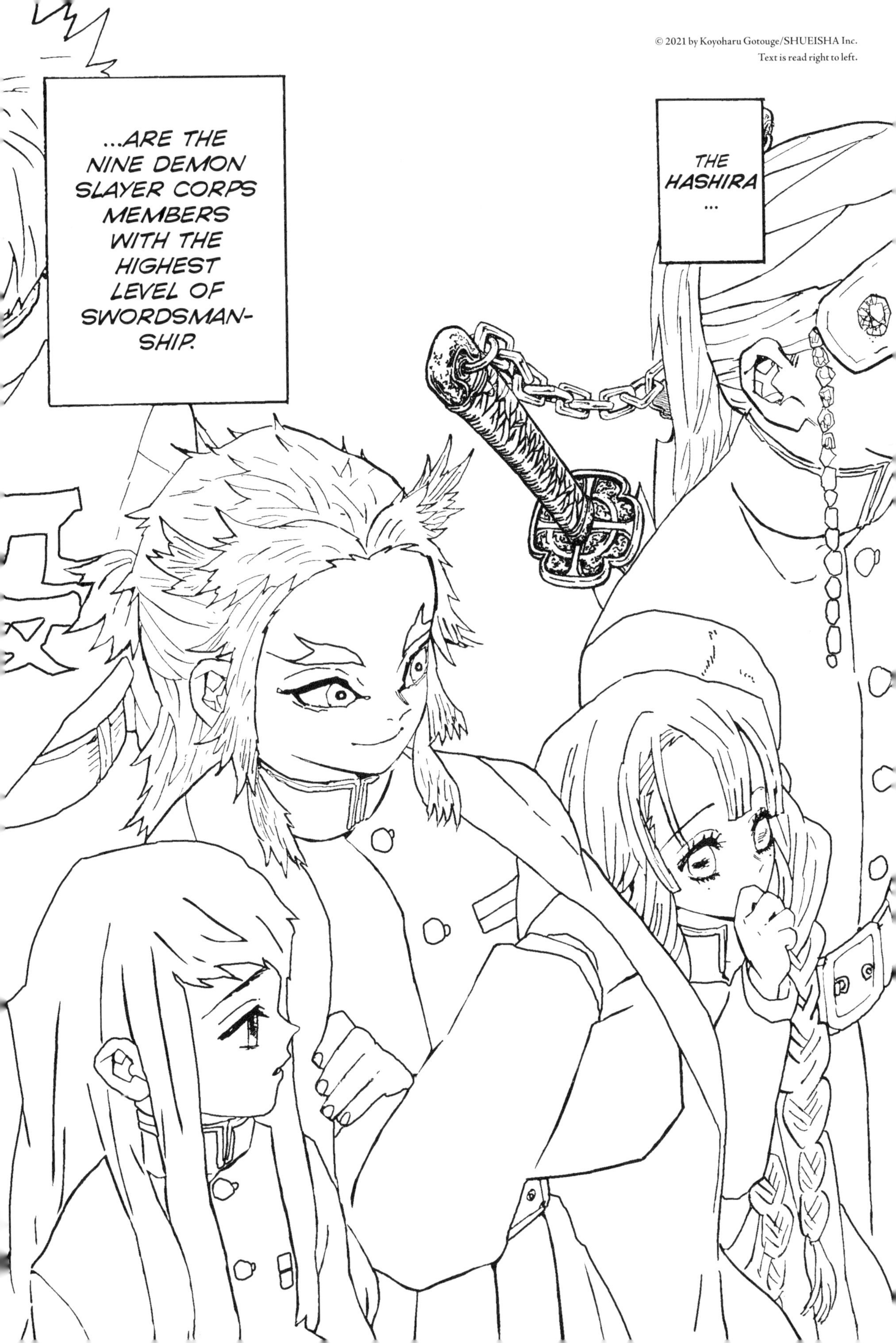
THE HASHIRA...
...ARE THE NINE DEMON SLAYER CORPS MEMBERS WITH THE HIGHEST LEVEL OF SWORDSMANSHIP.

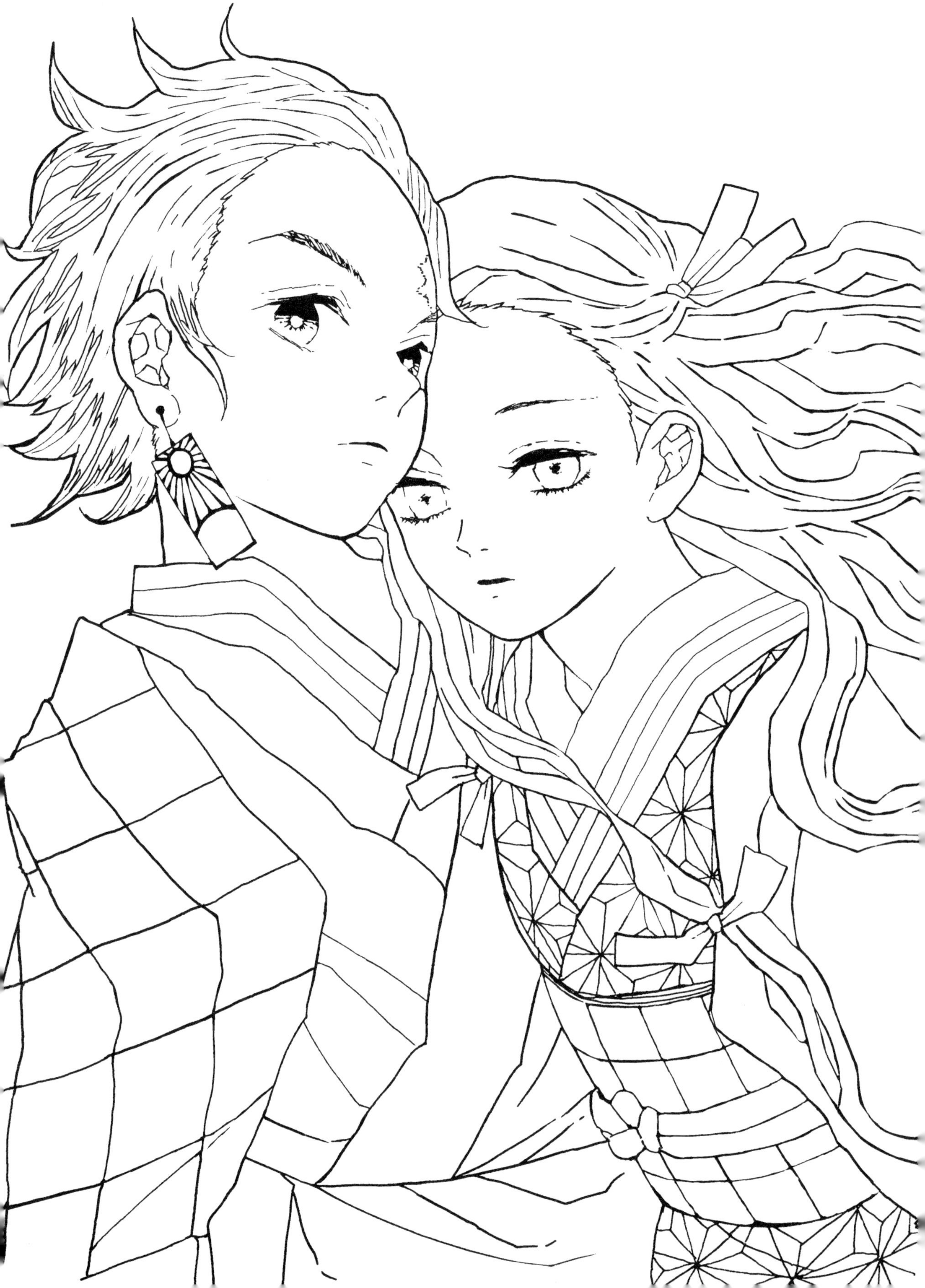

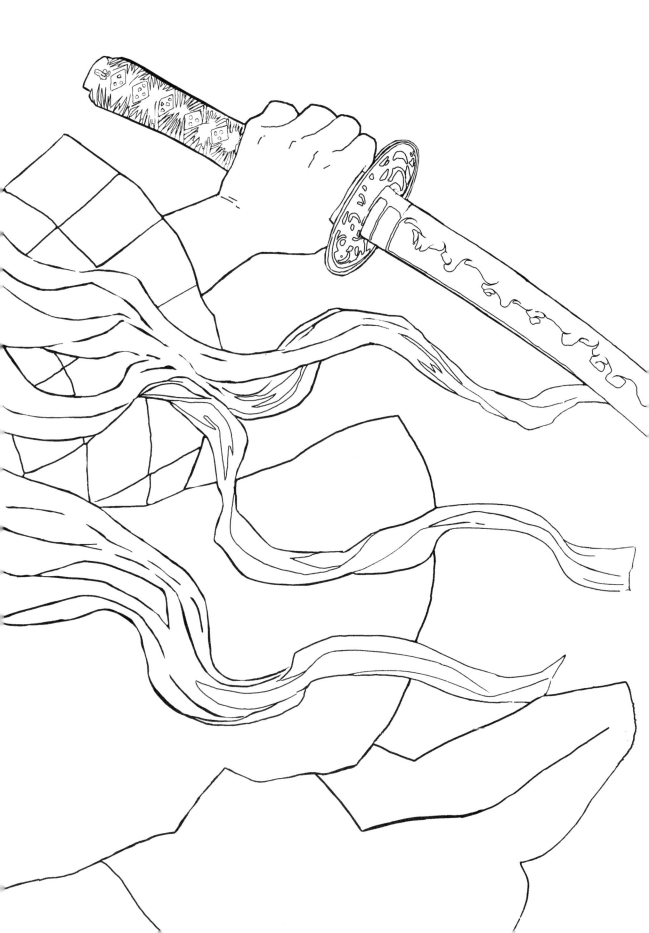

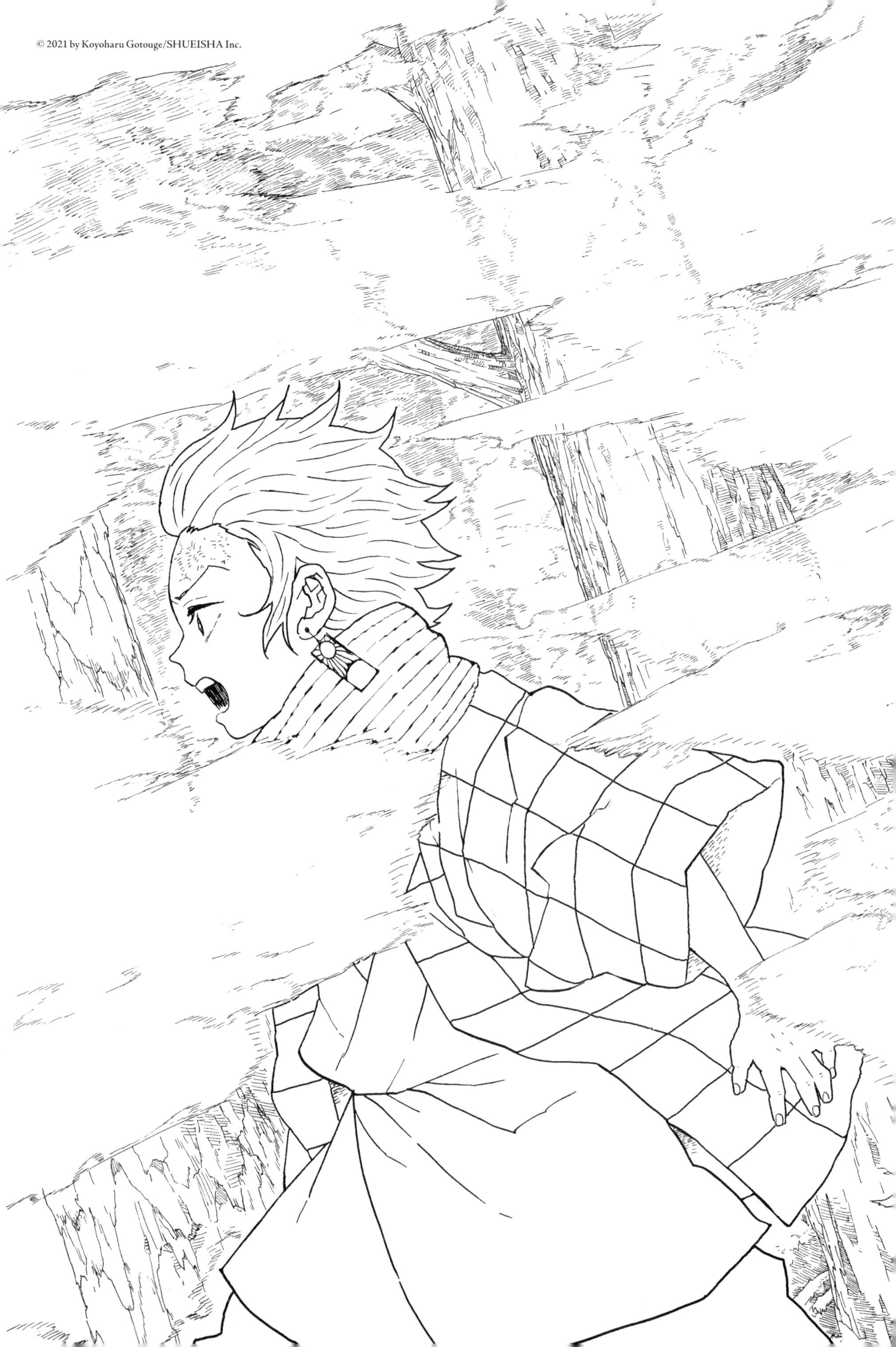

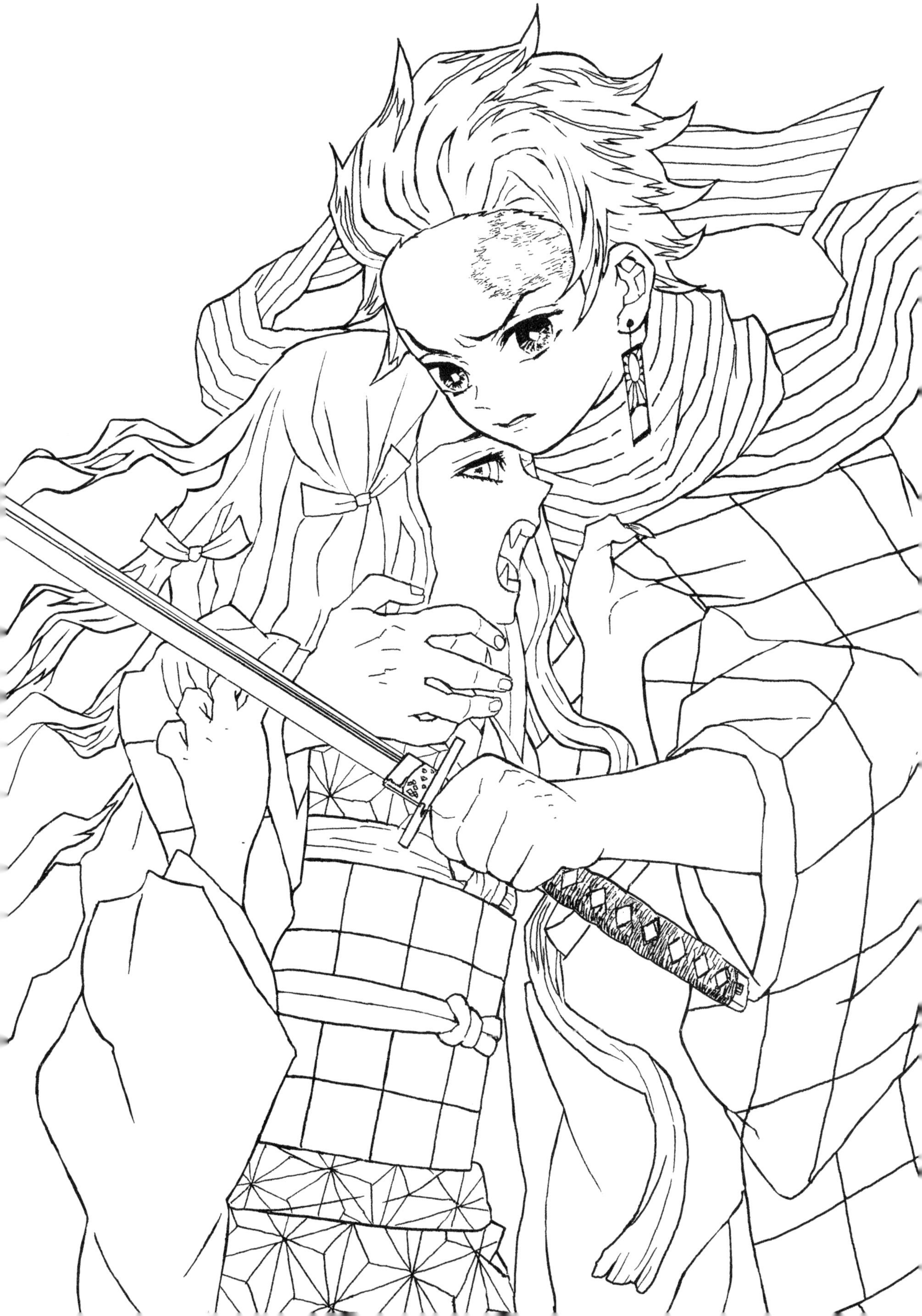

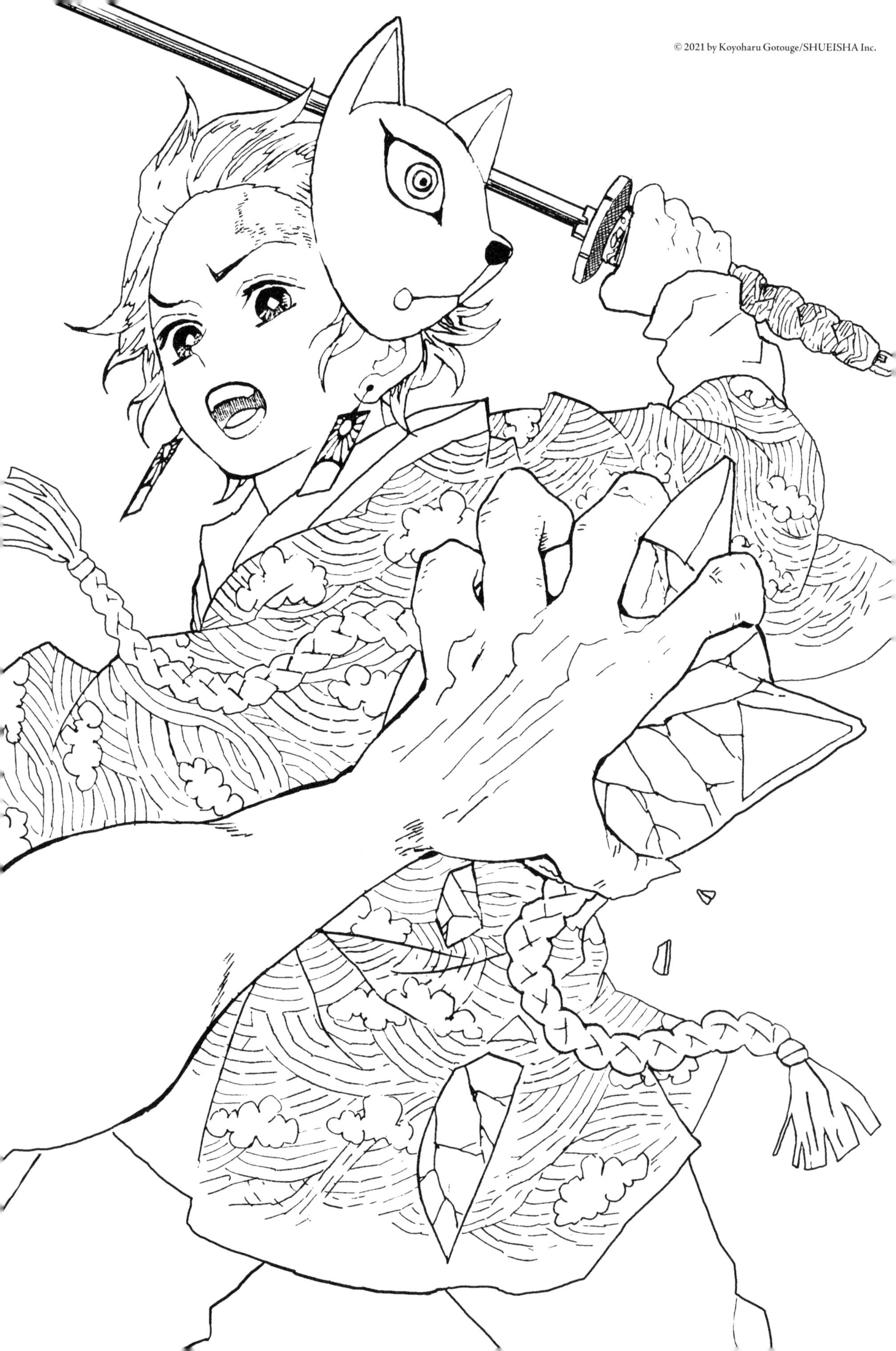

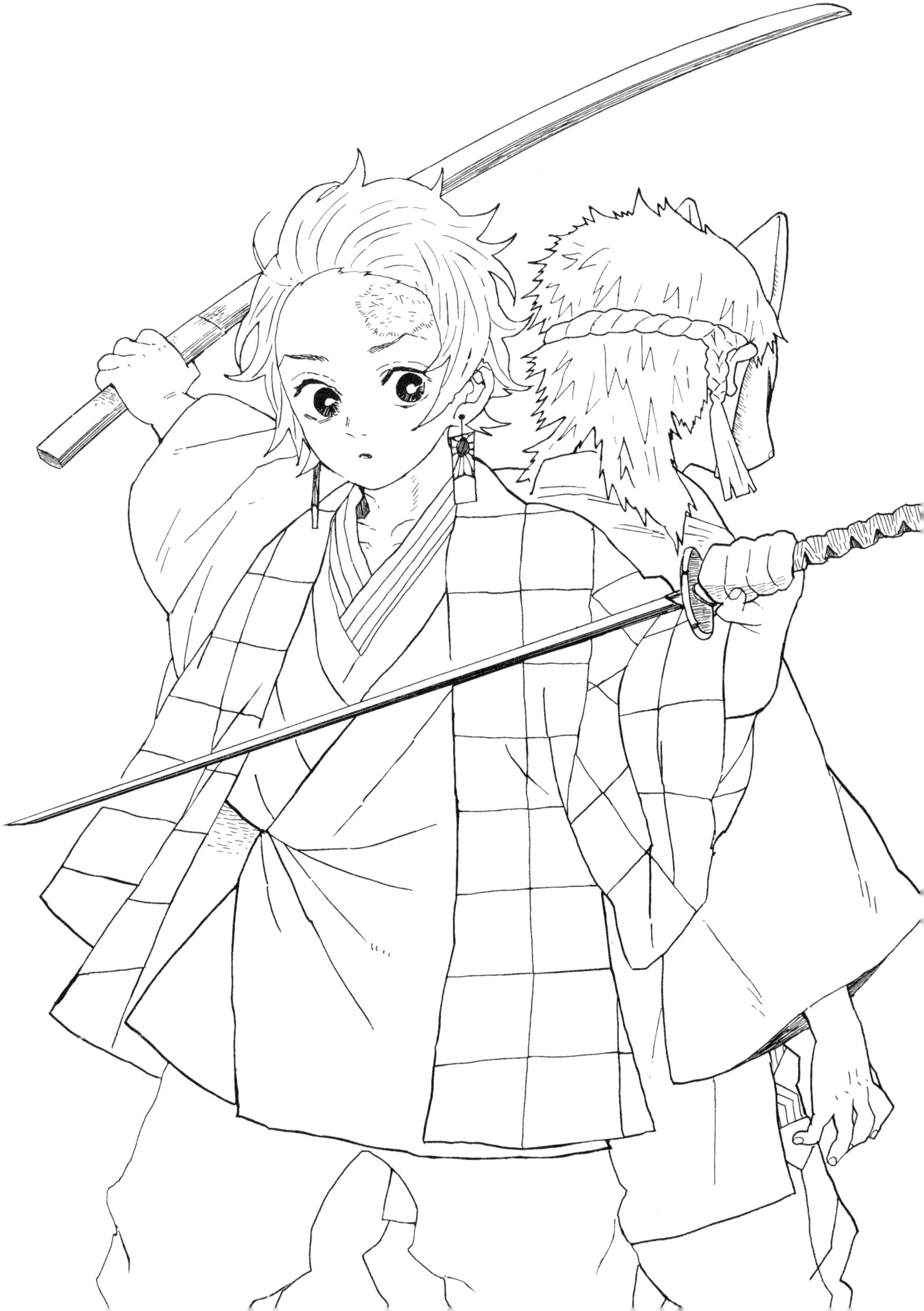

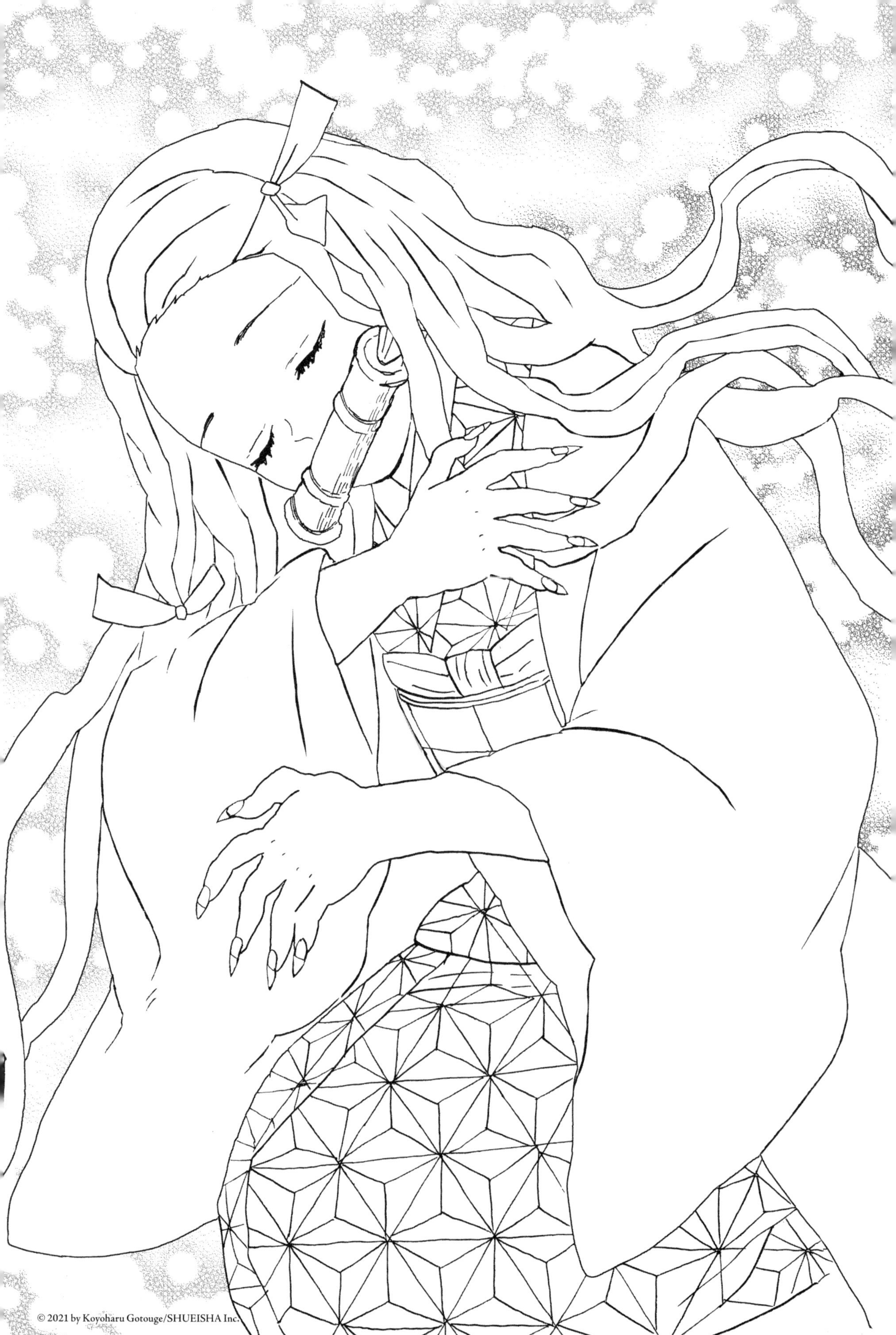

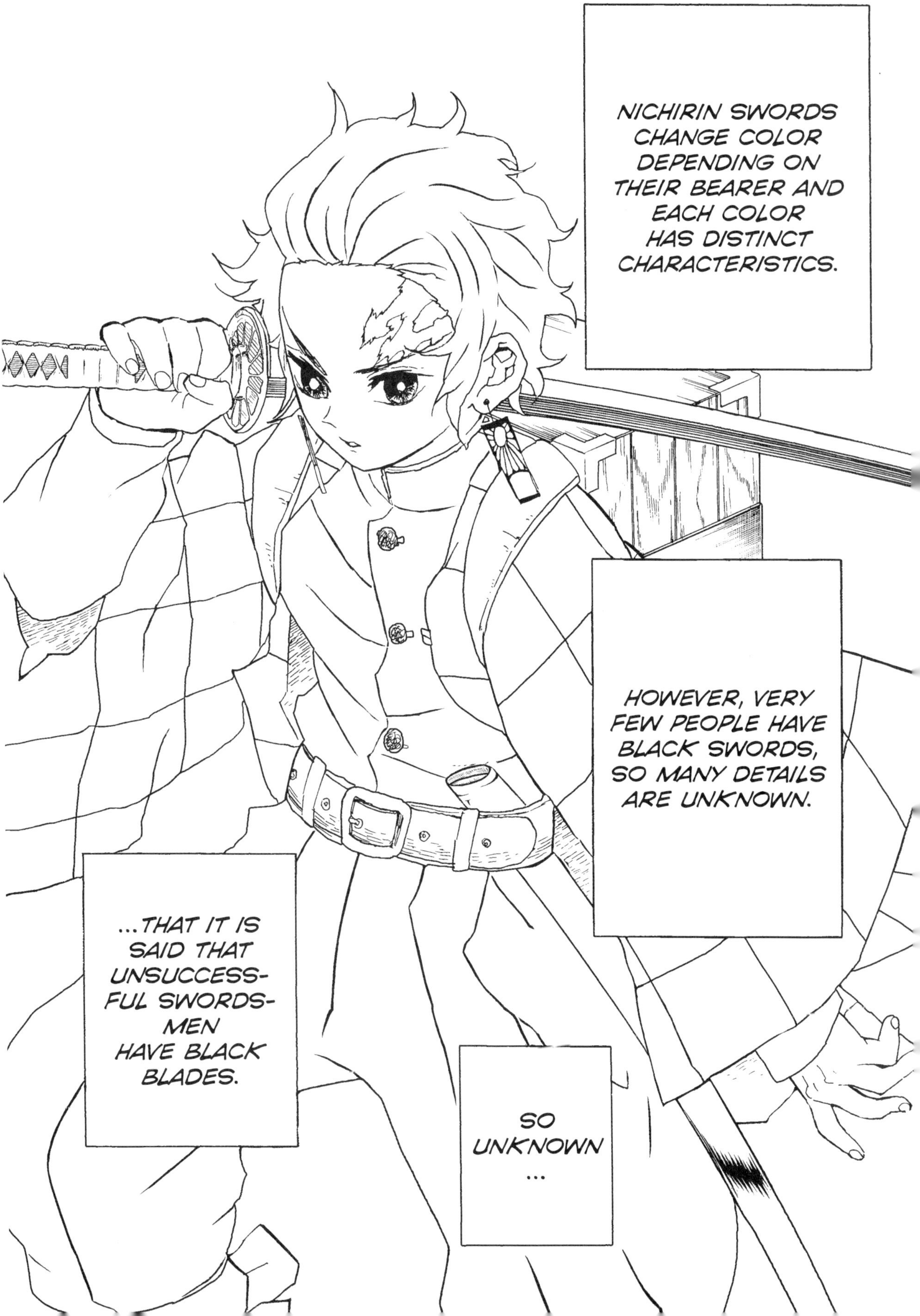
NICHIRIN SWORDS CHANGE COLOR DEPENDING ON THEIR BEARER AND EACH COLOR HAS DISTINCT CHARACTERISTICS.
HOWEVER, VERY FEW PEOPLE HAVE BLACK SWORDS, SO MANY DETAILS ARE UNKNOWN.
SO UNKNOWN …
…THAT IT IS SAID THAT UNSUCCESS-FUL SWORDS-MEN HAVE BLACK BLADES.

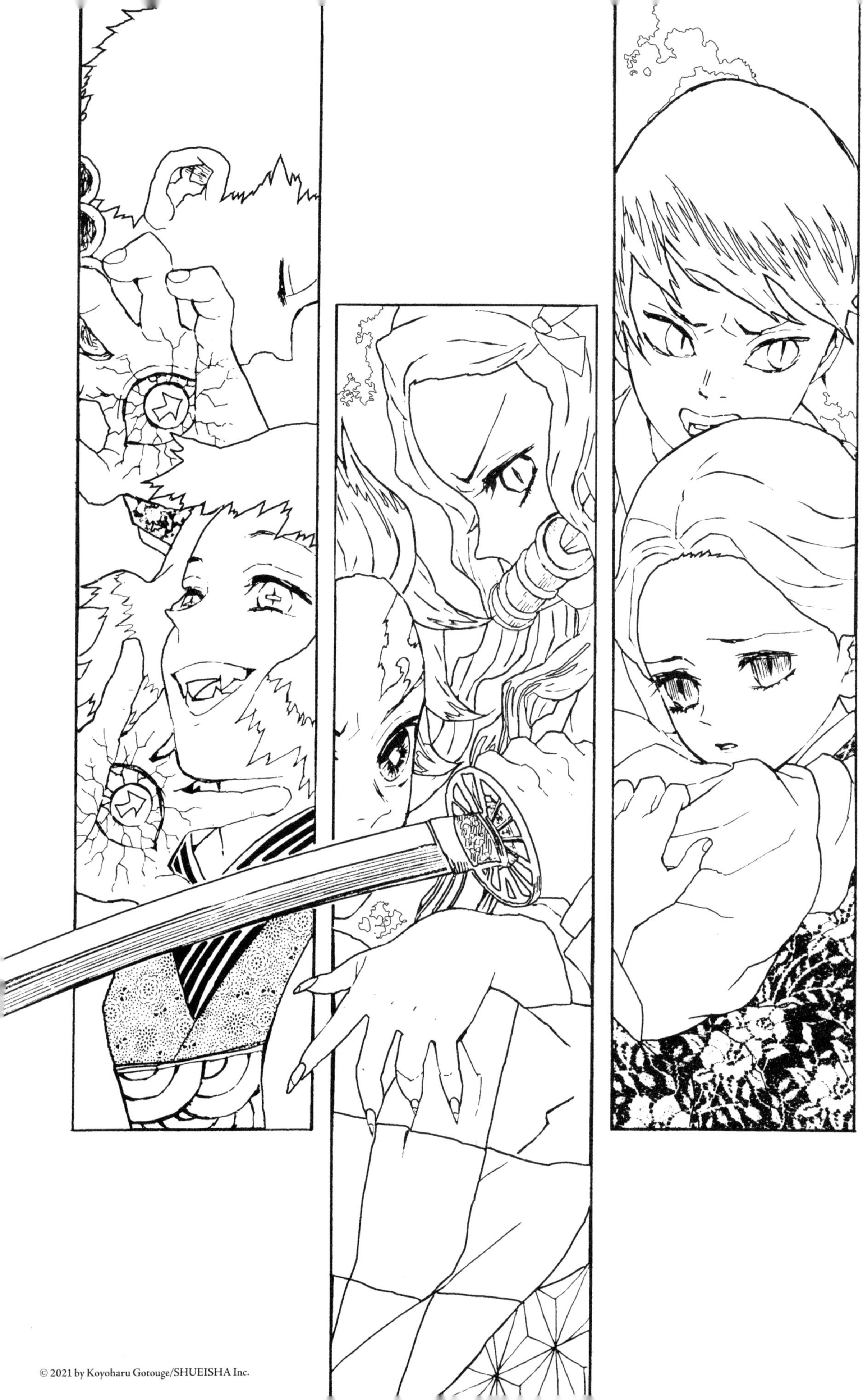

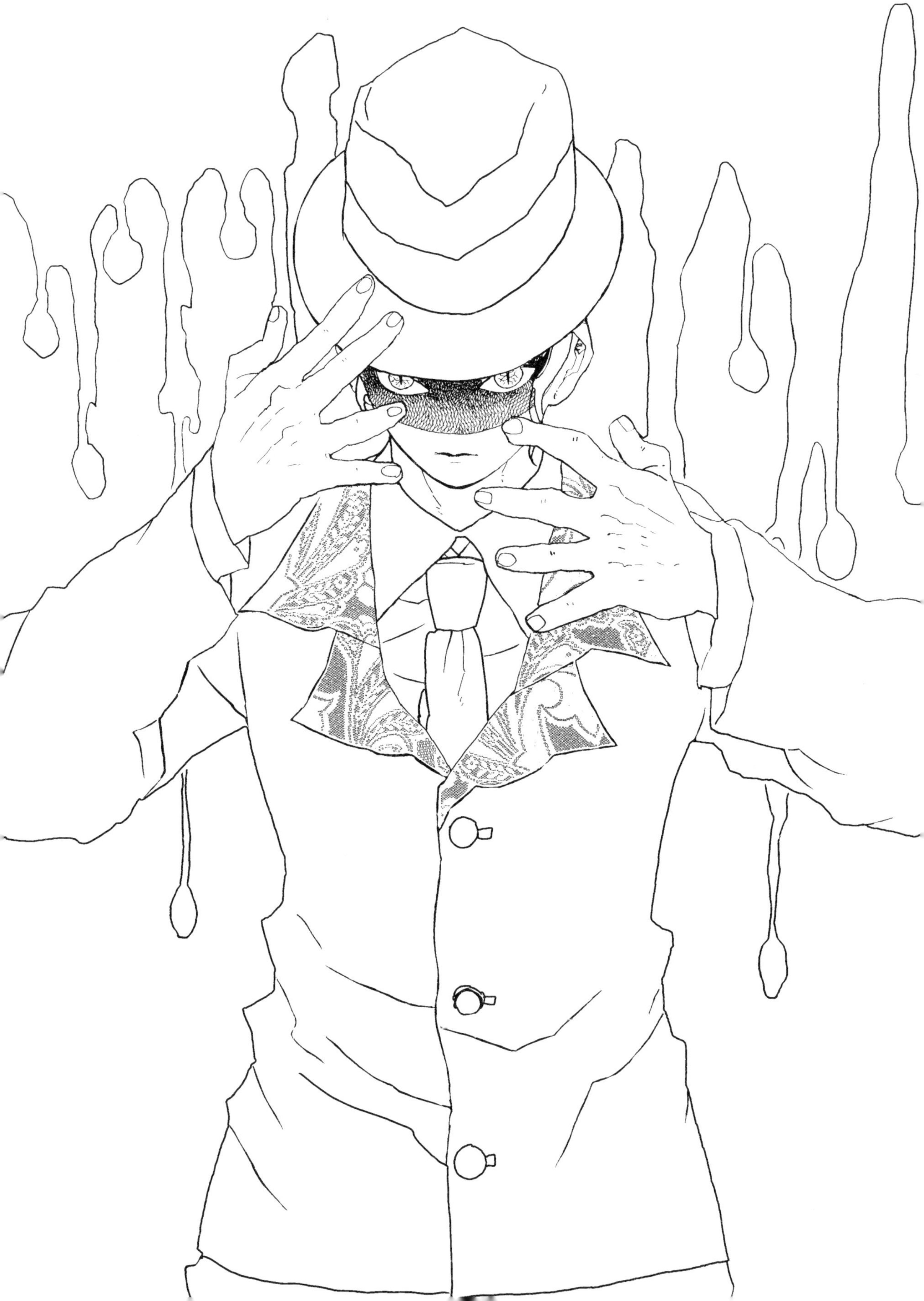

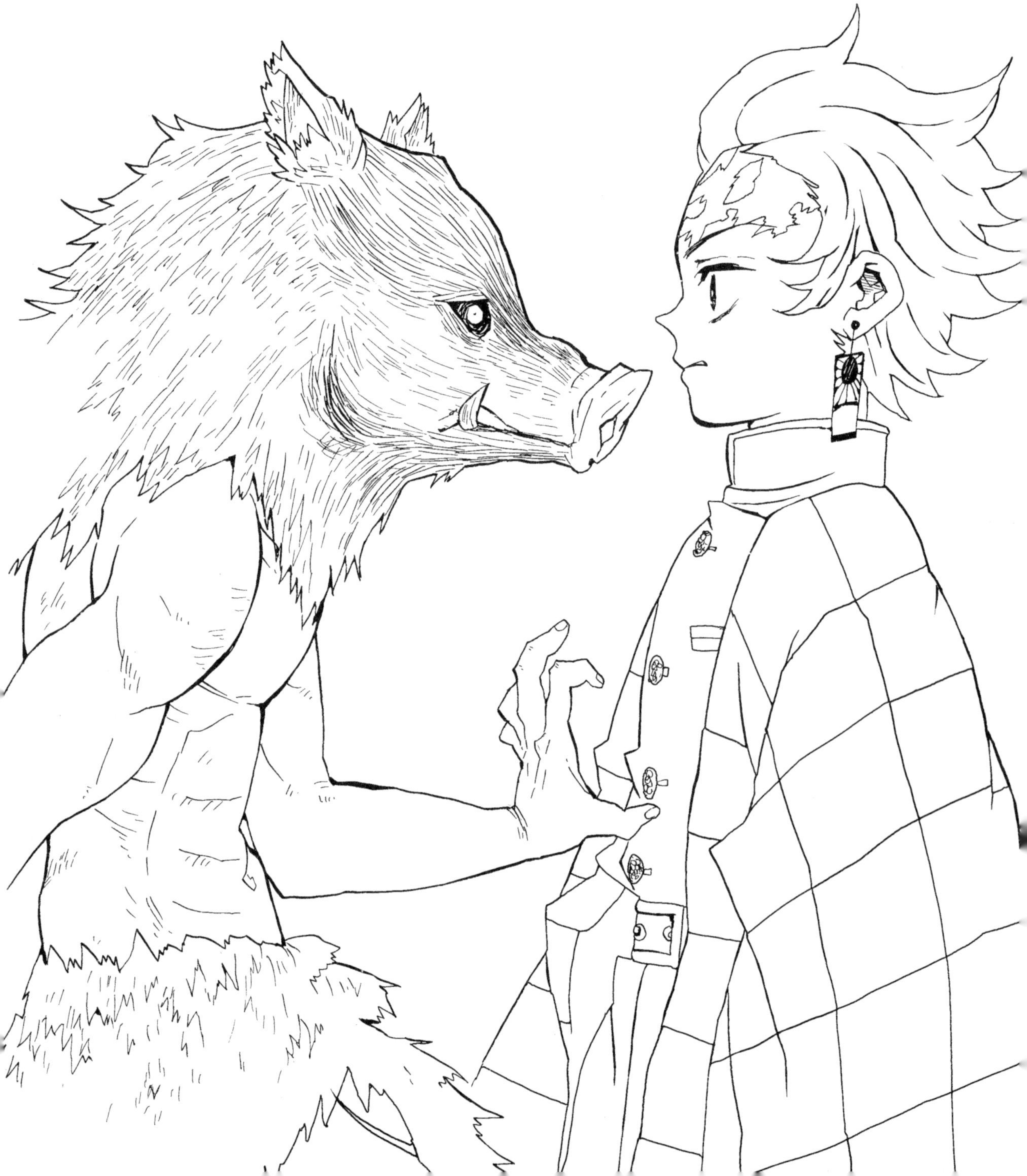

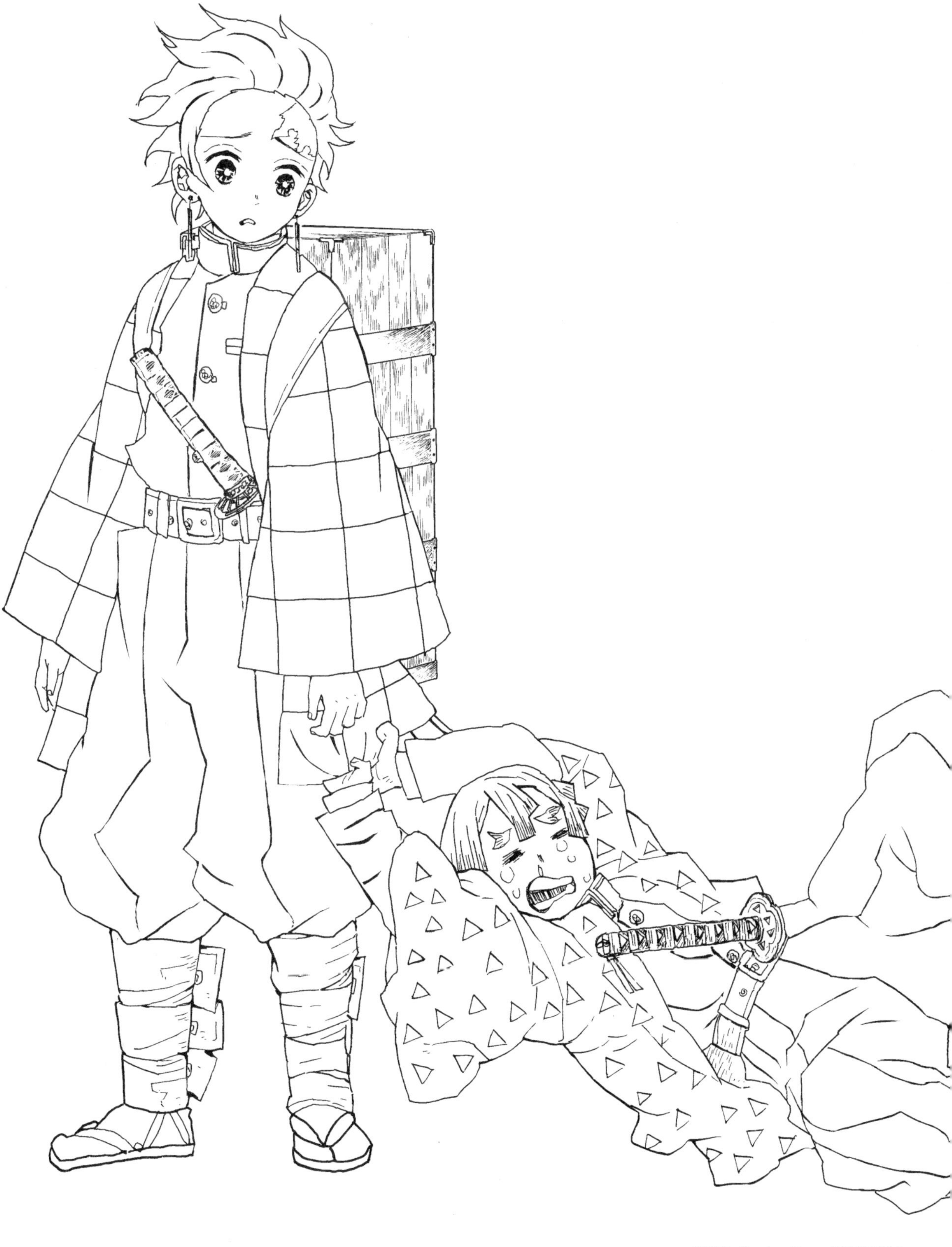

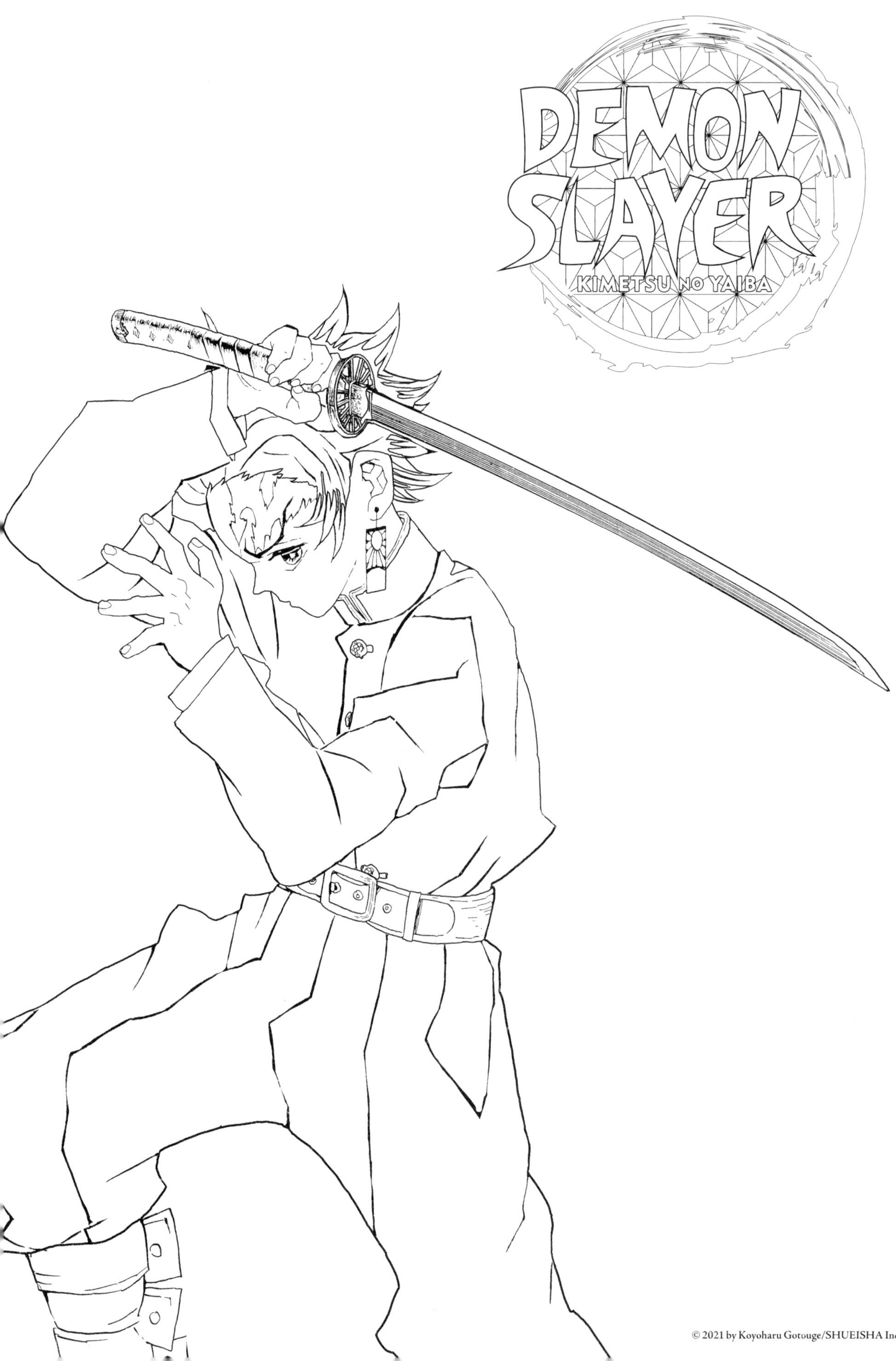
DEMON SLAYER
KIMETSU NO YAIBA

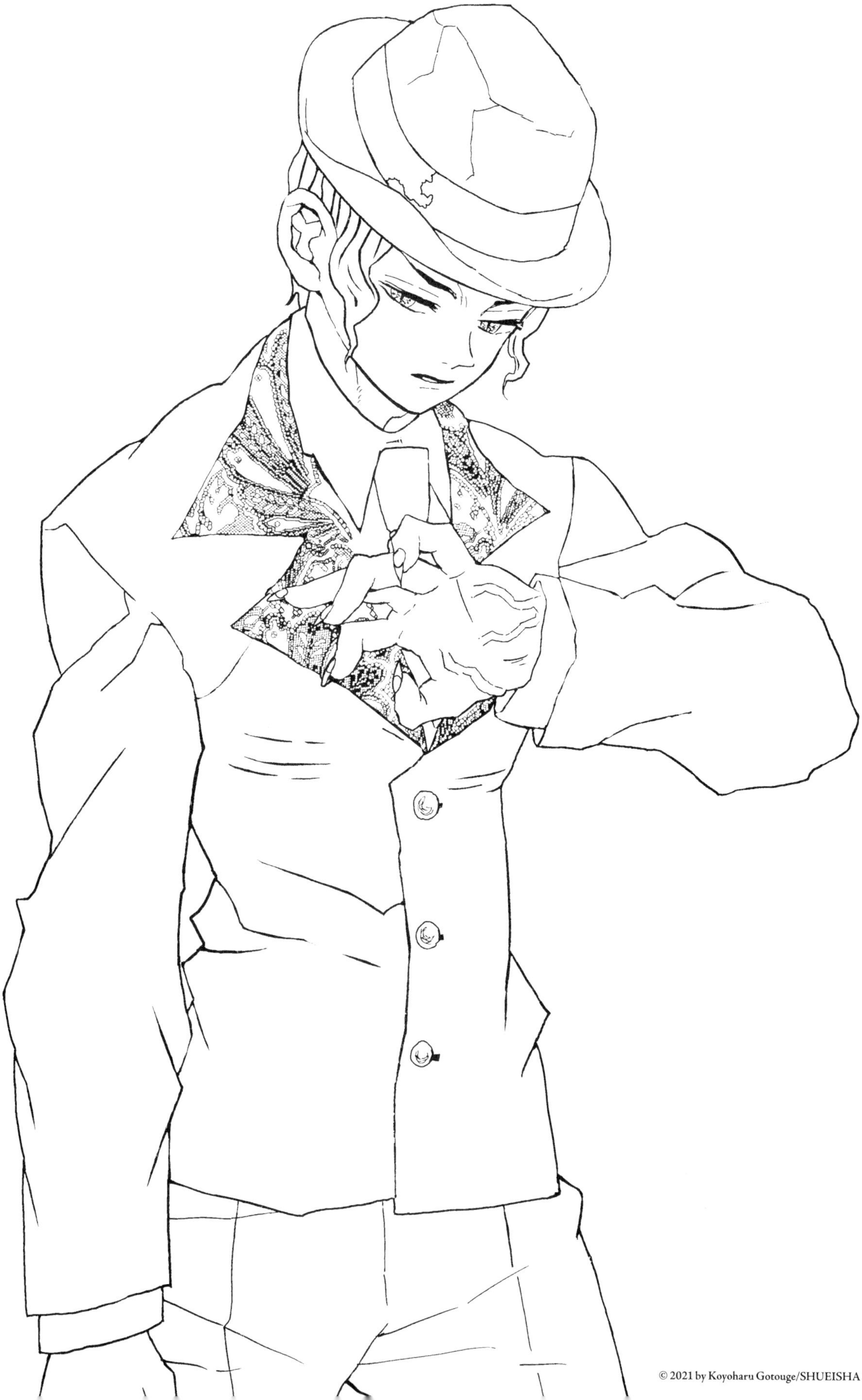

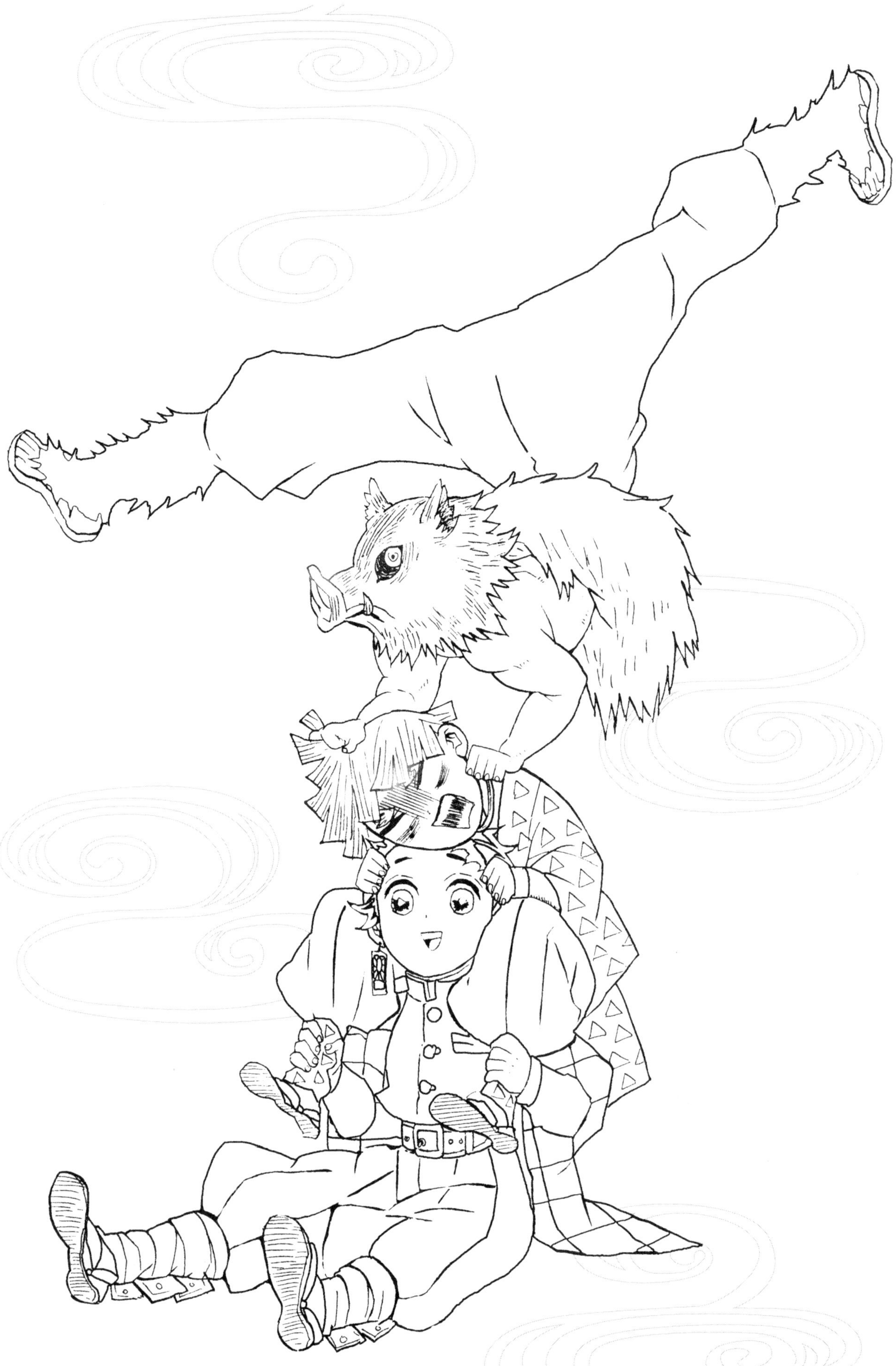

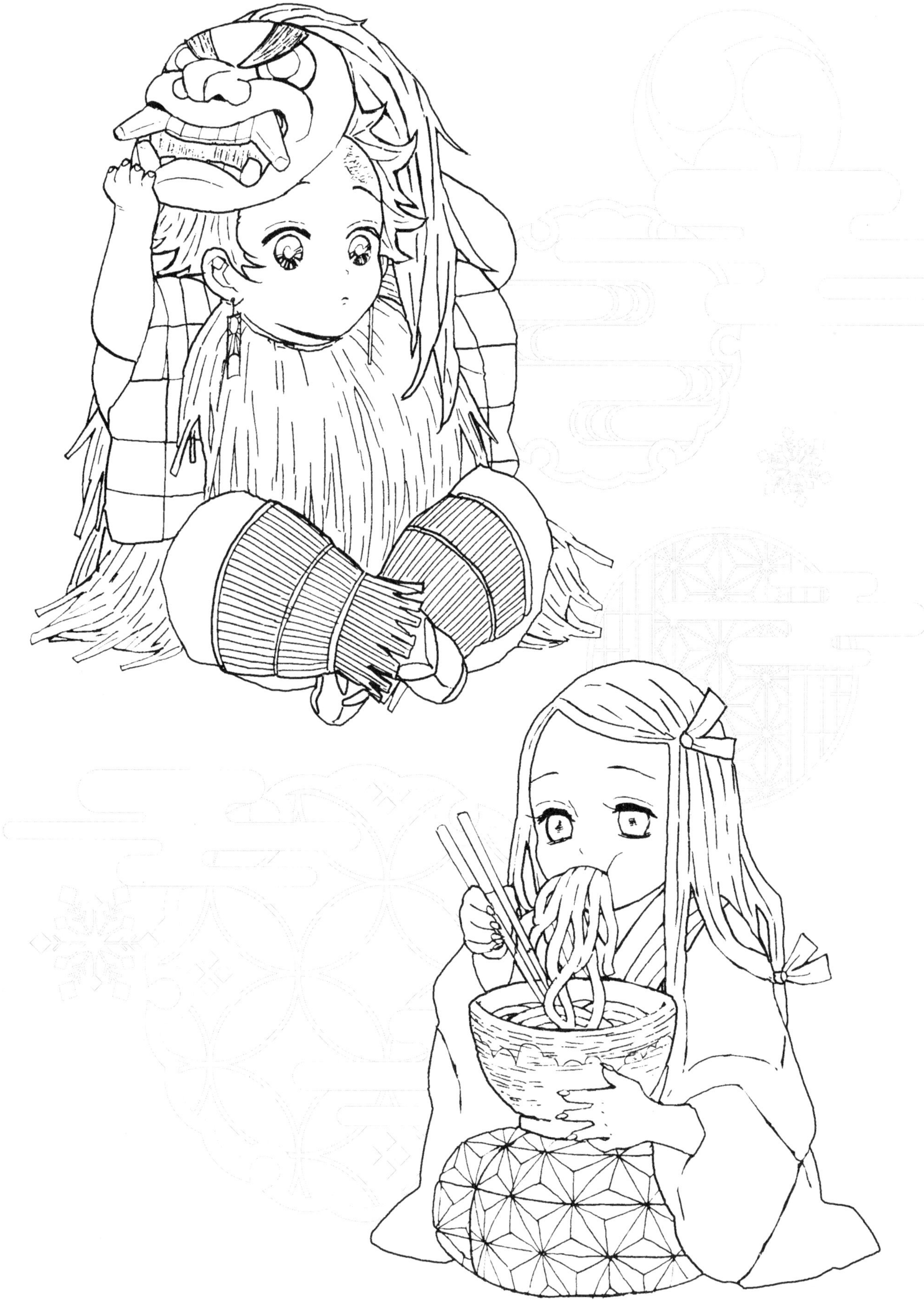

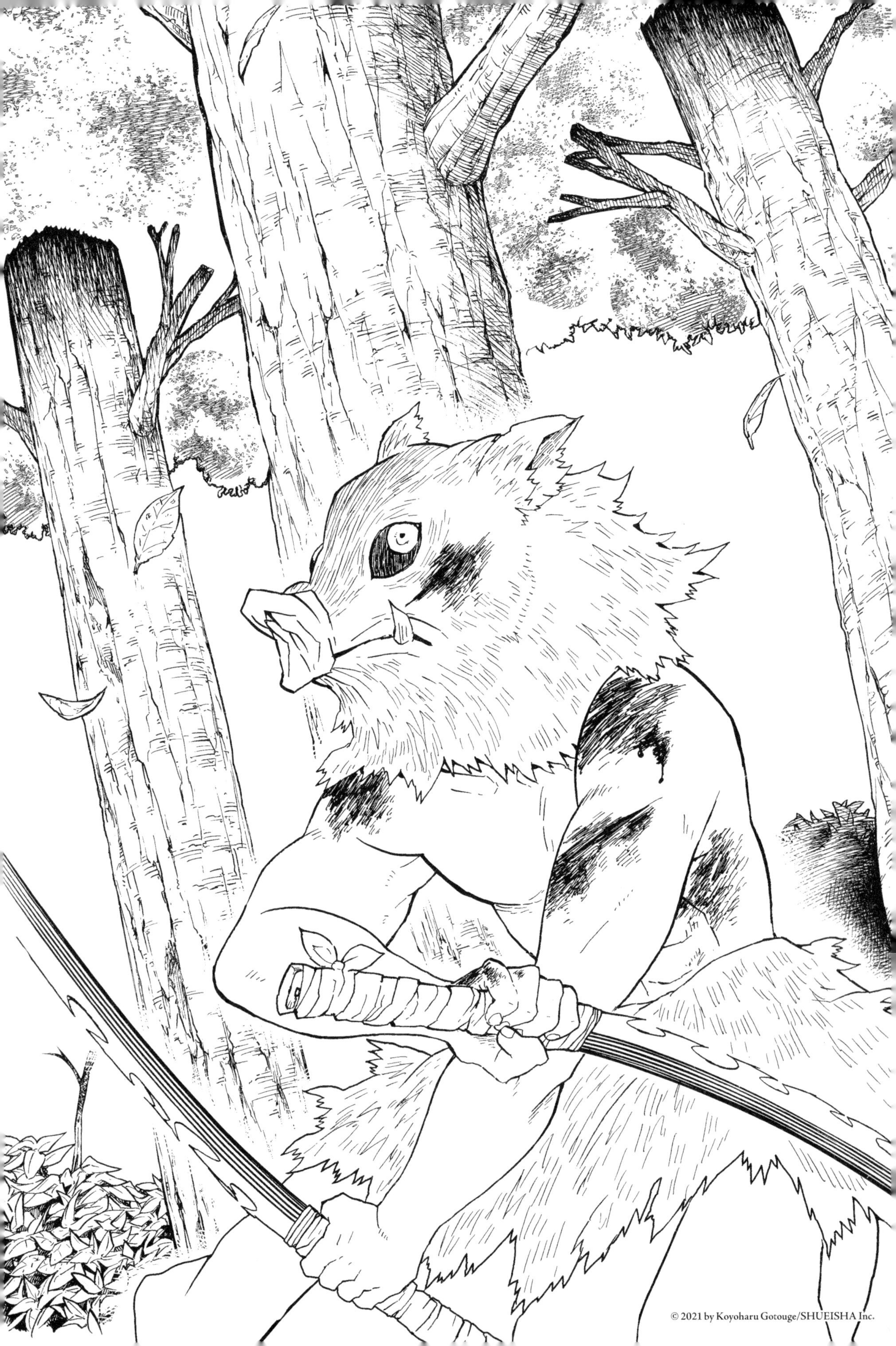

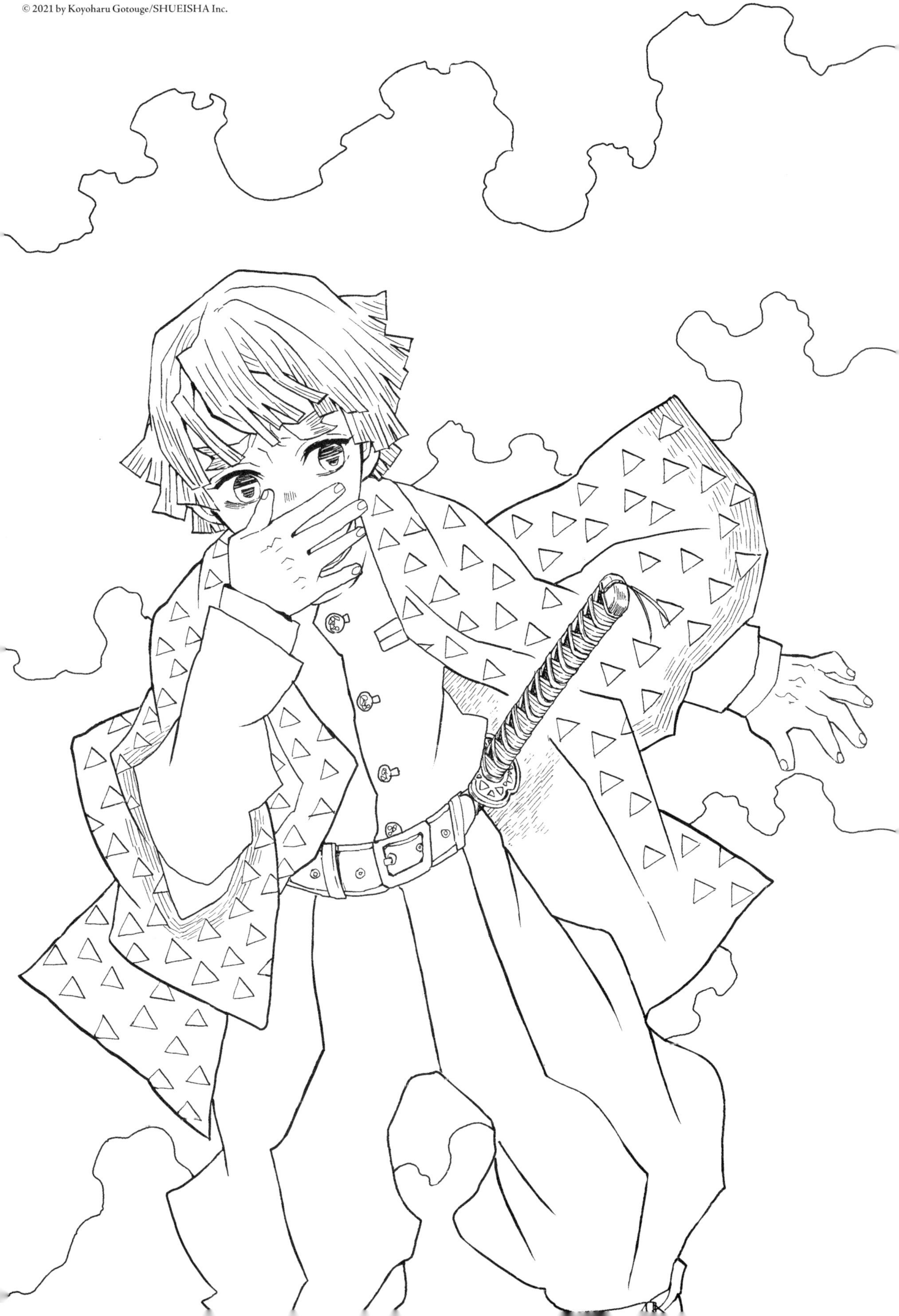

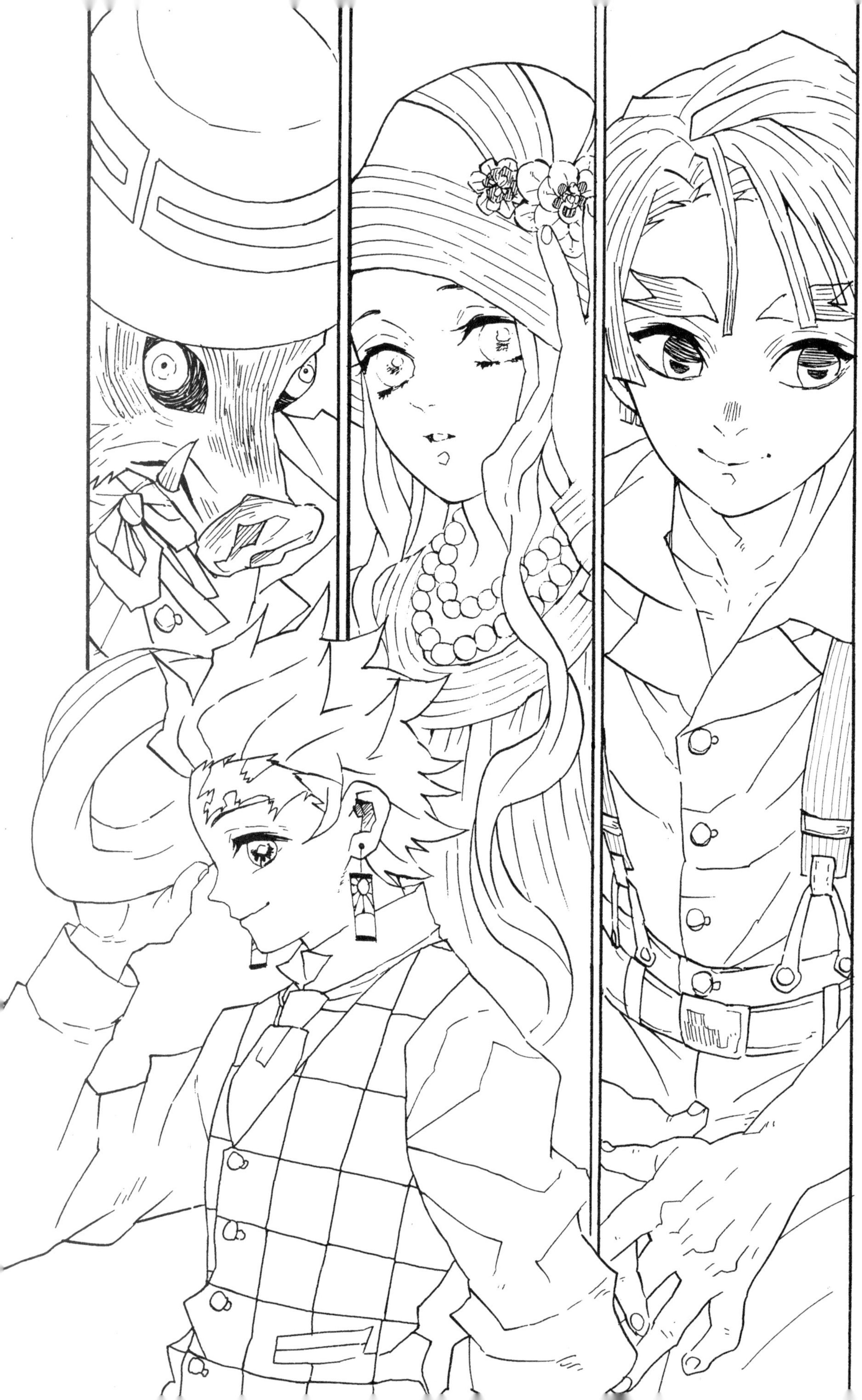

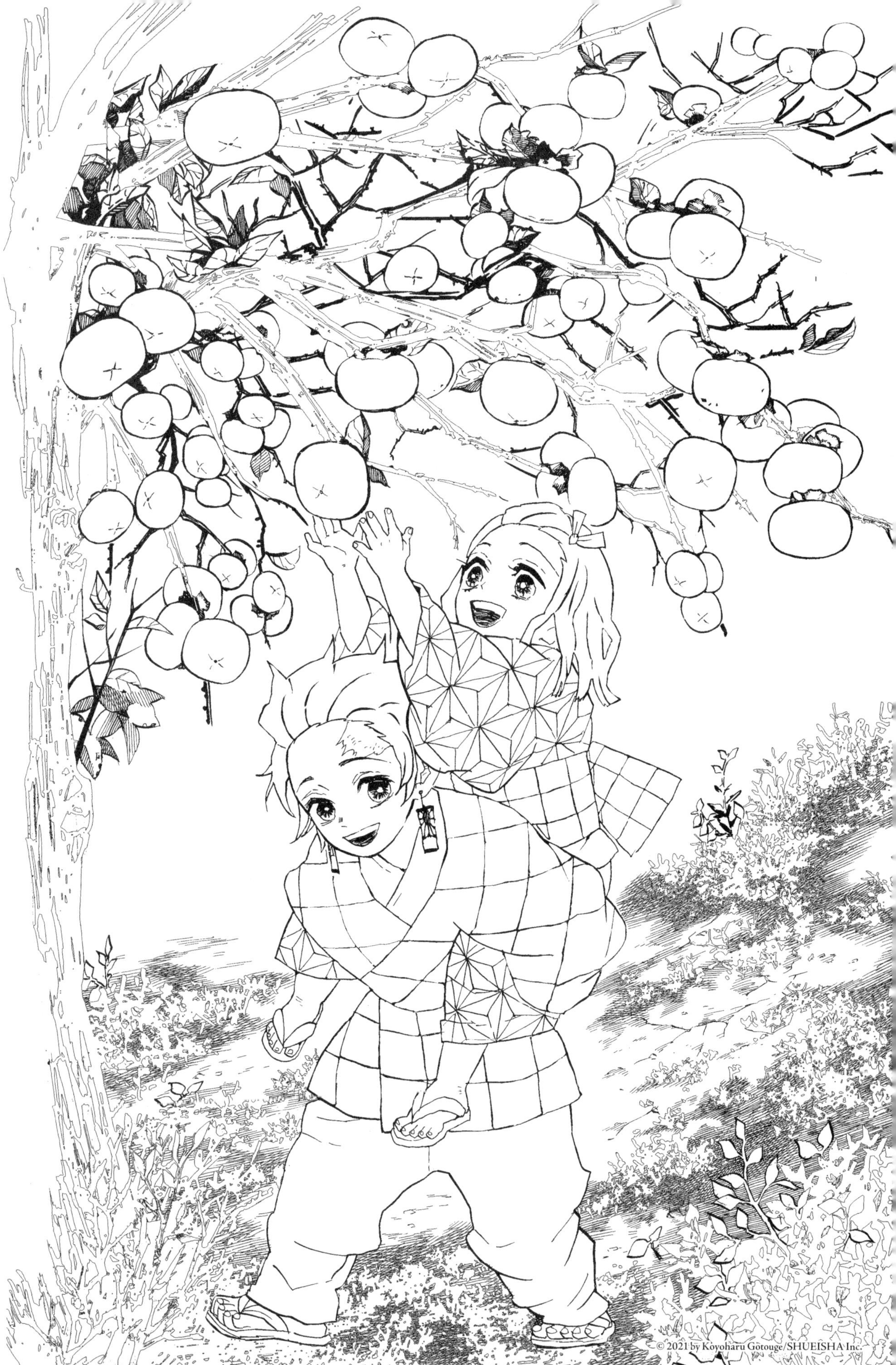

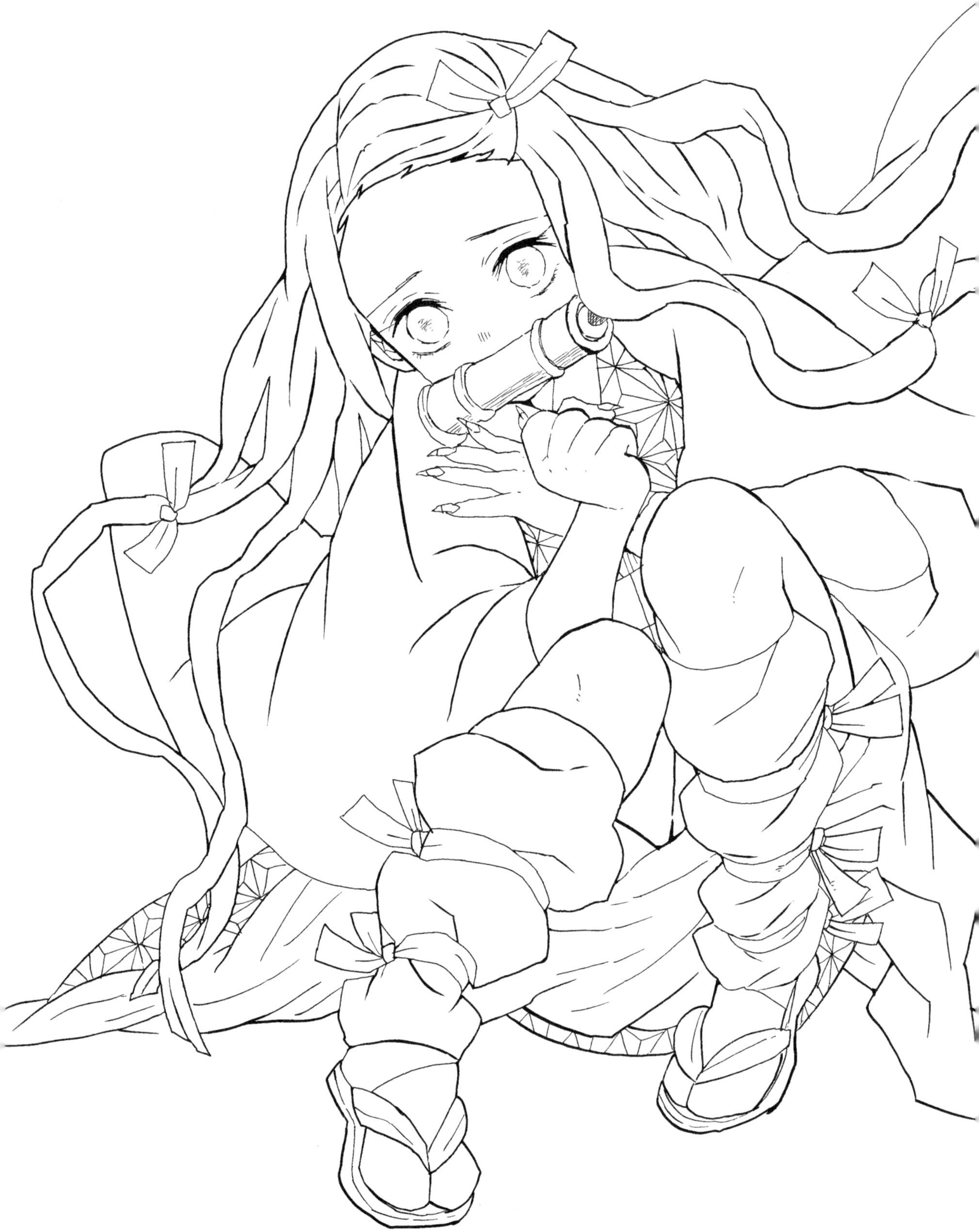

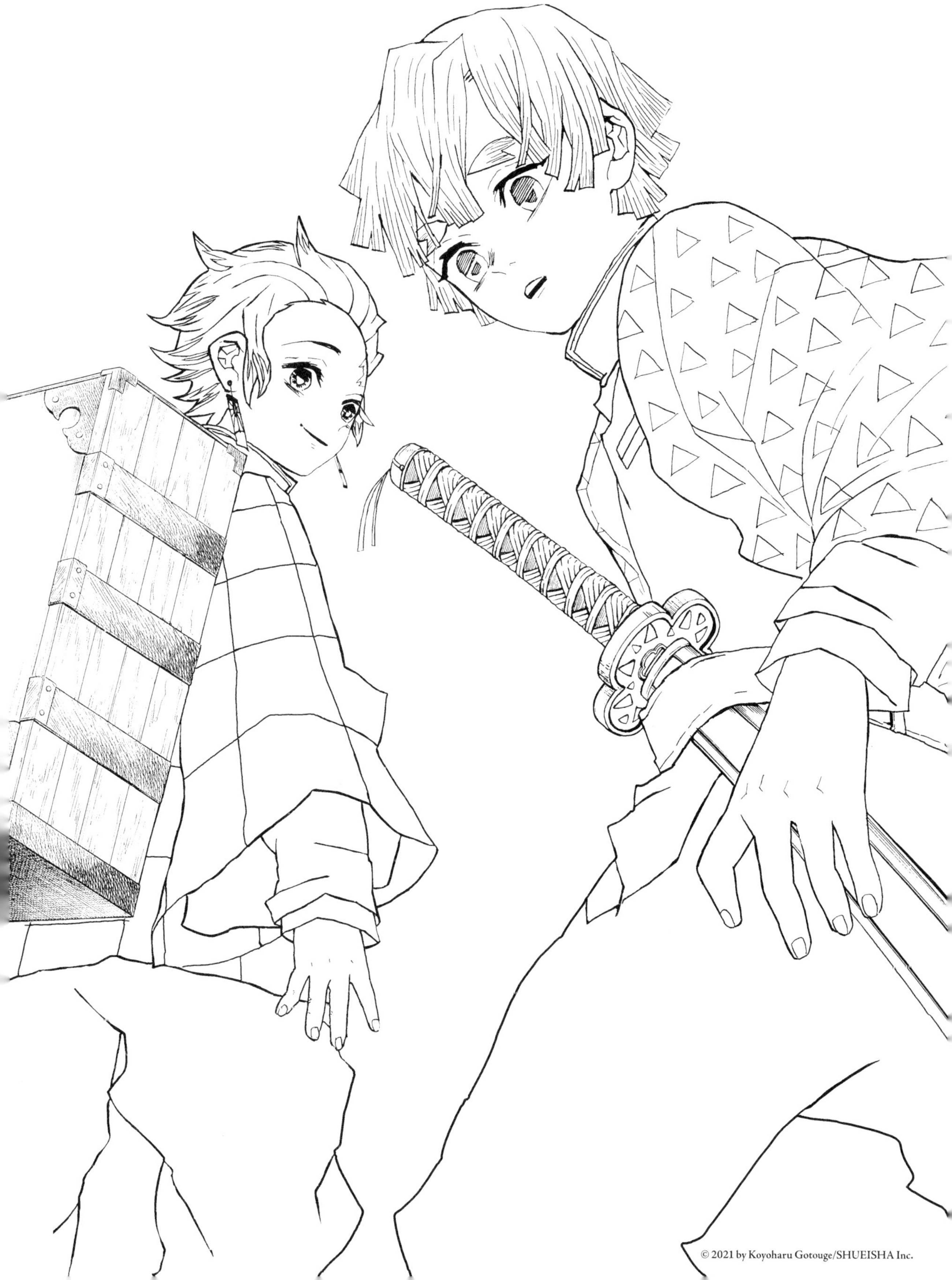

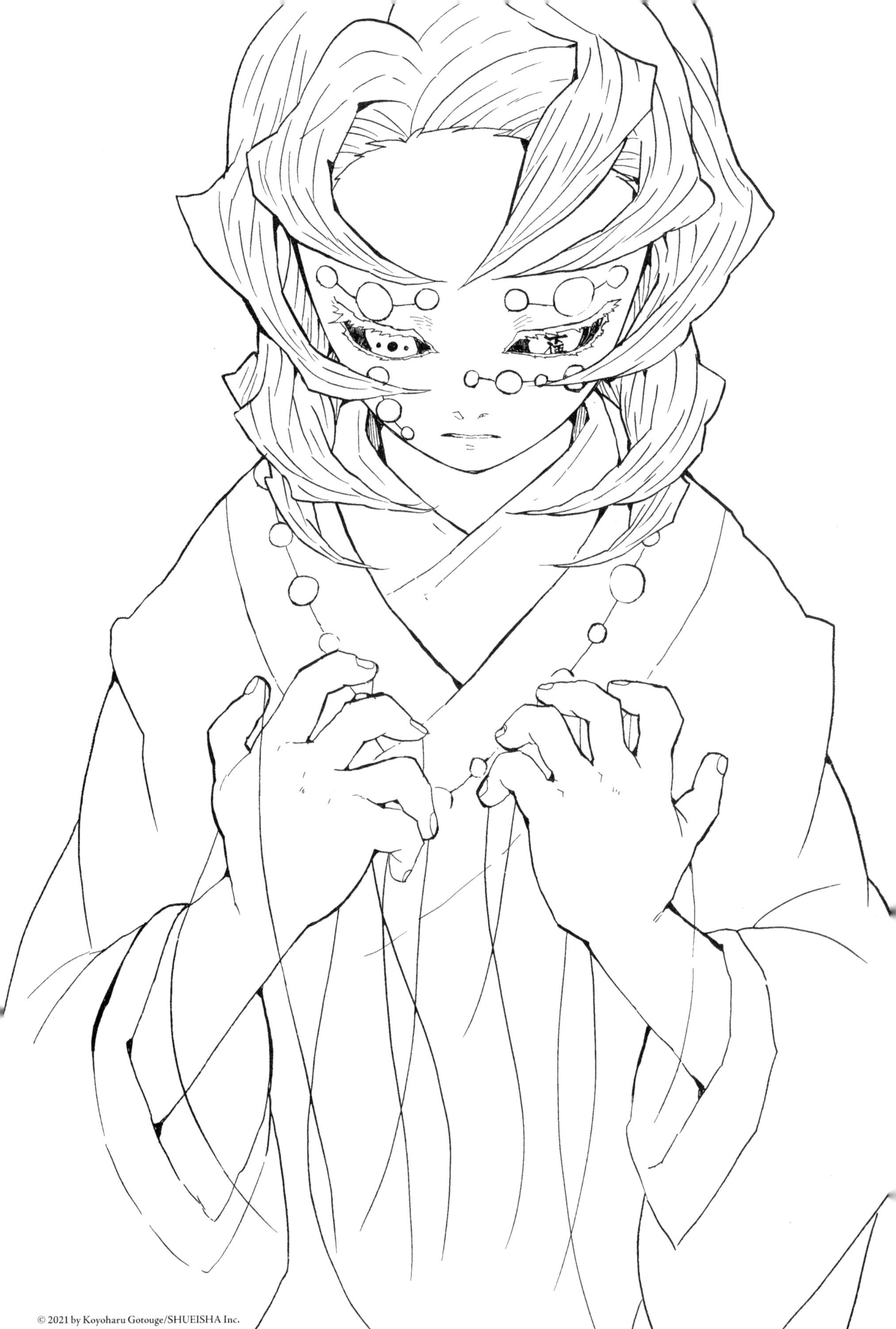

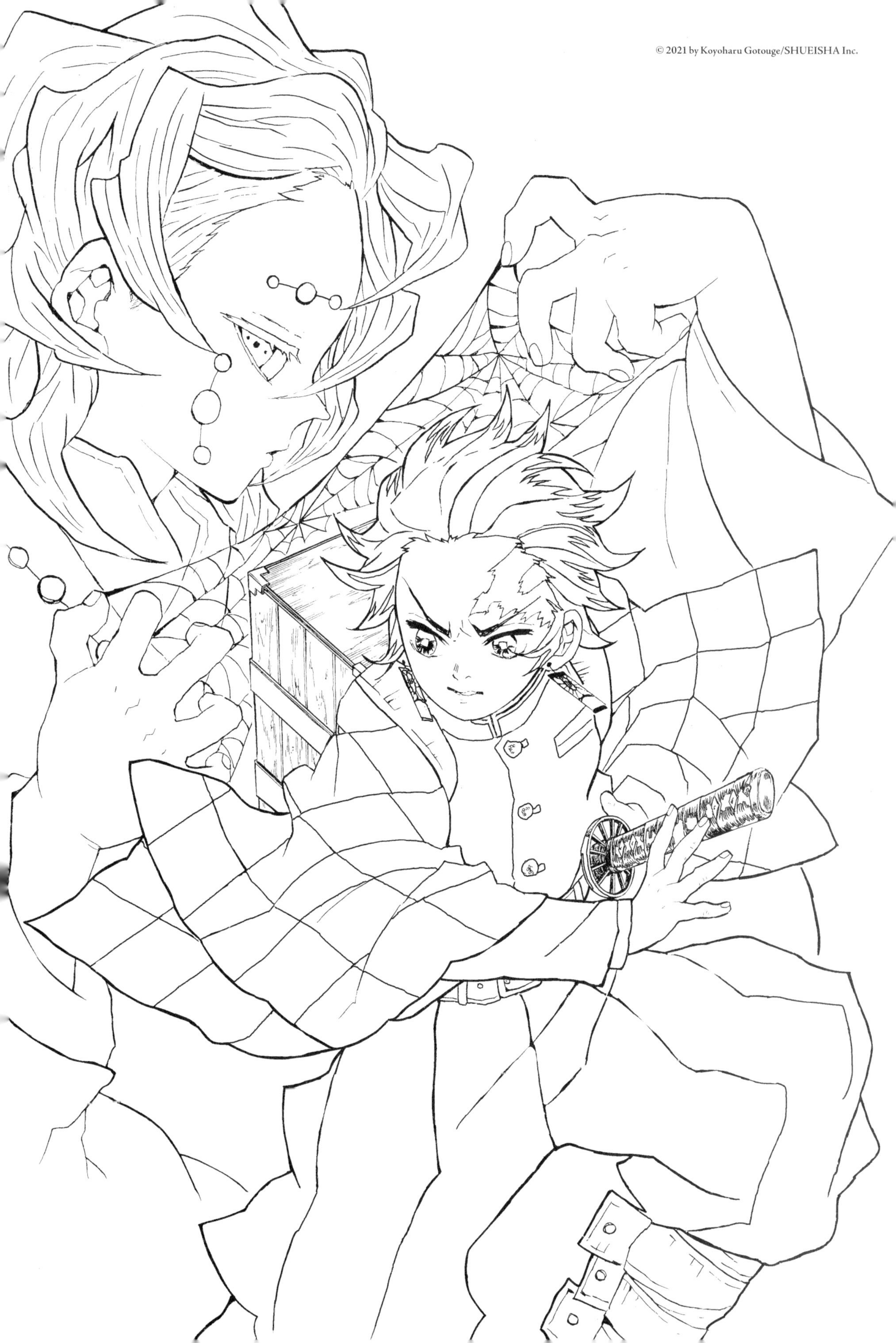

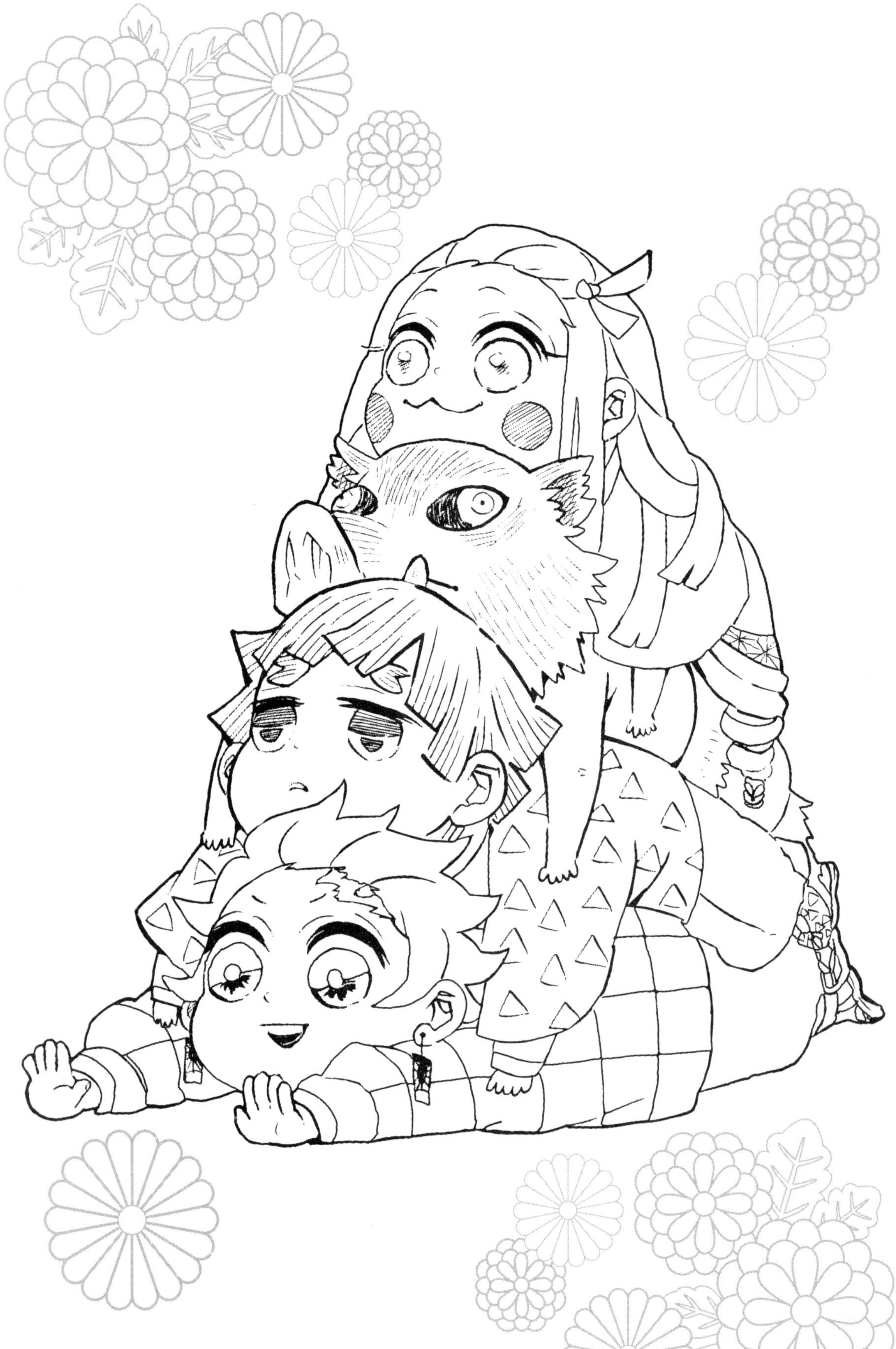

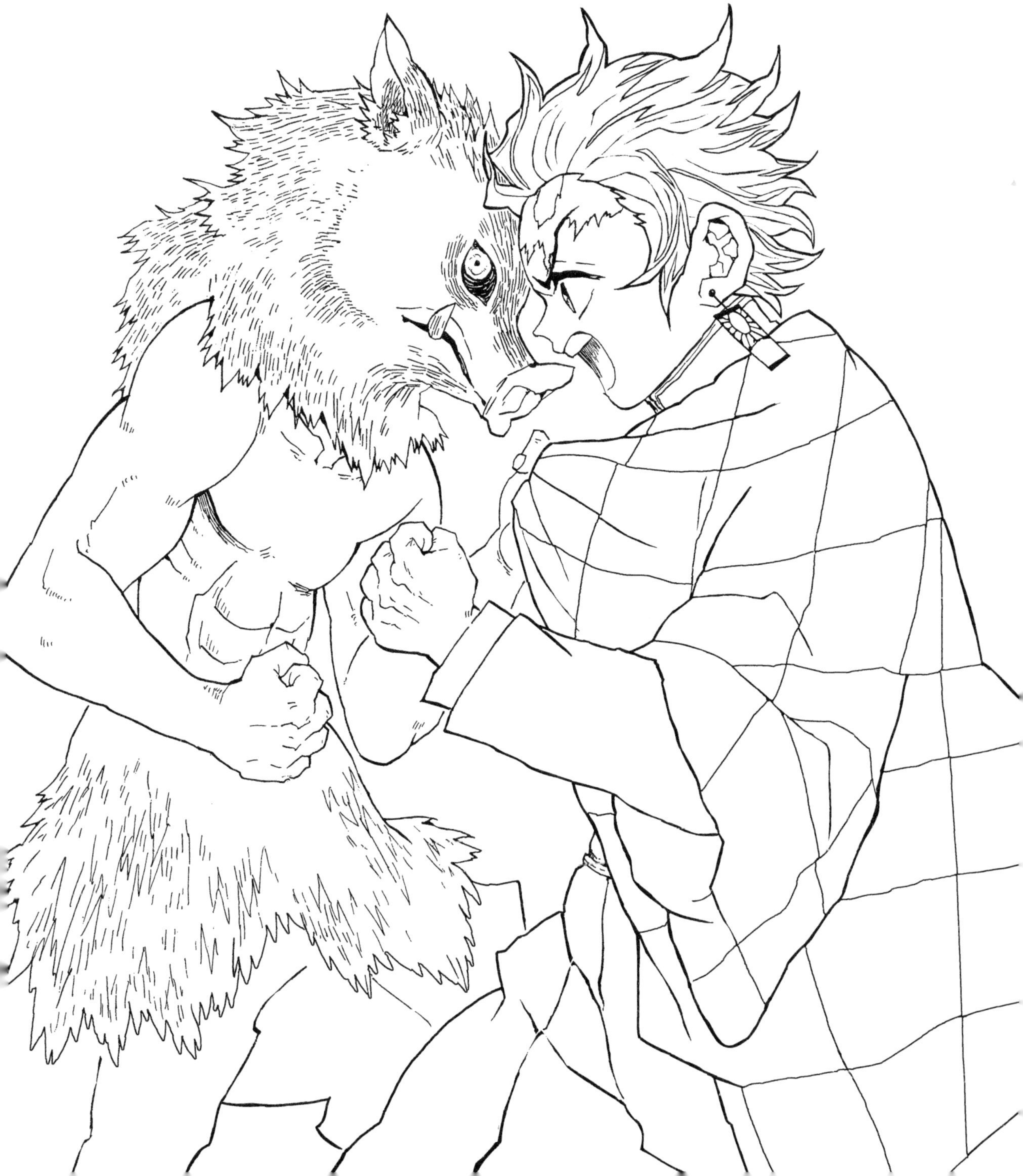

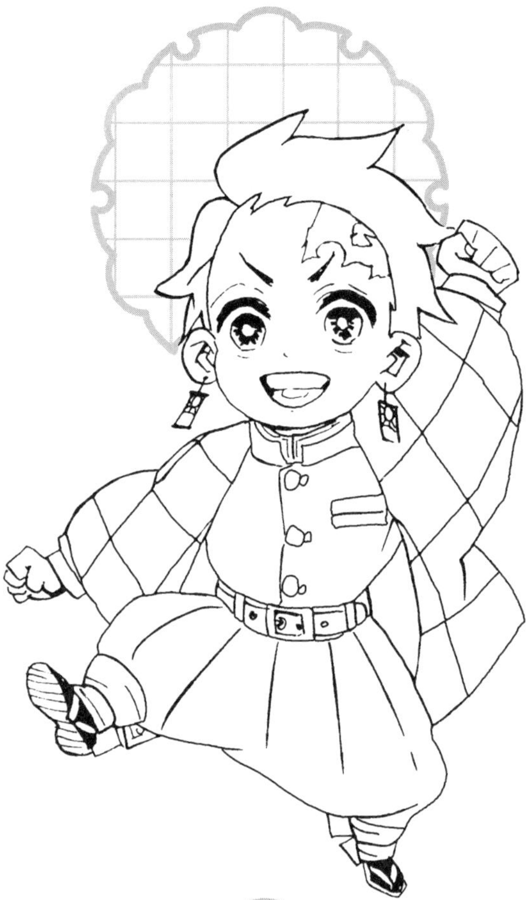
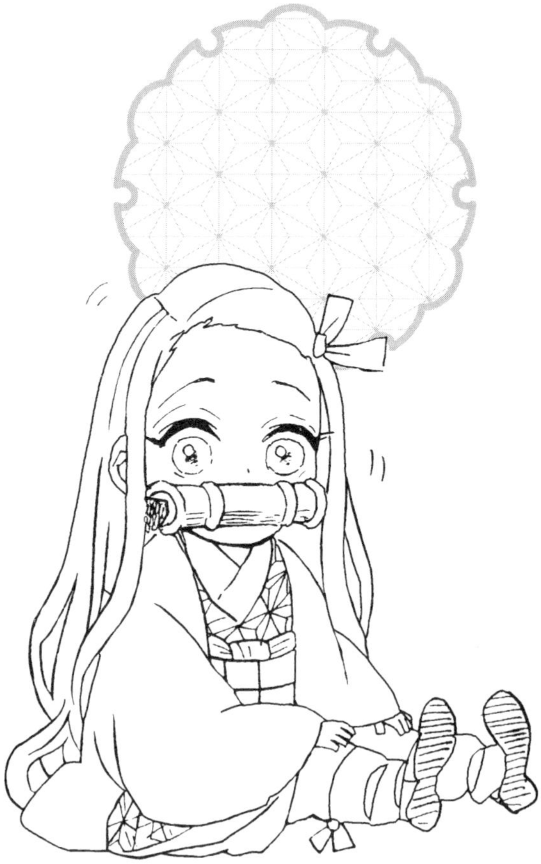
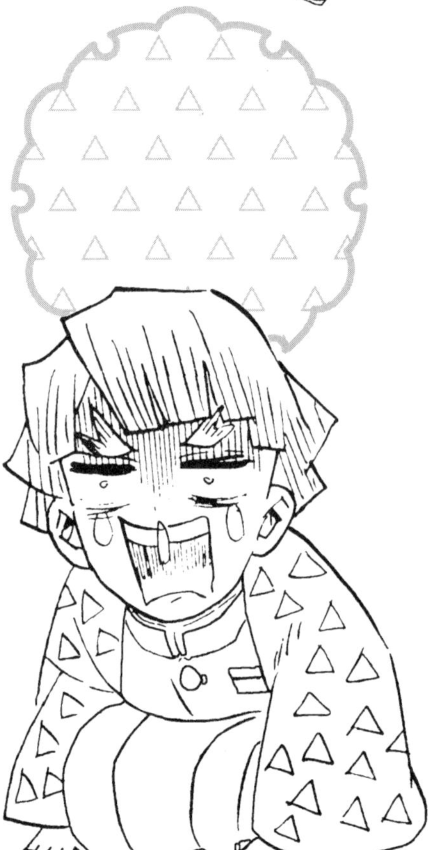
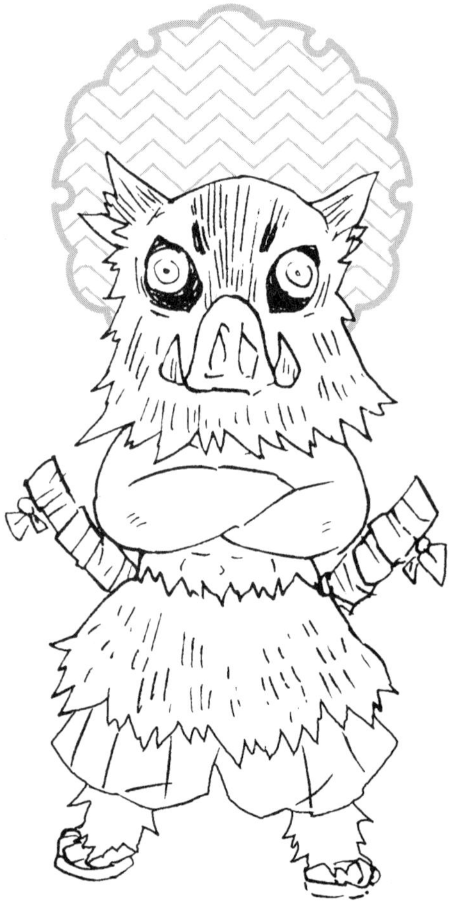

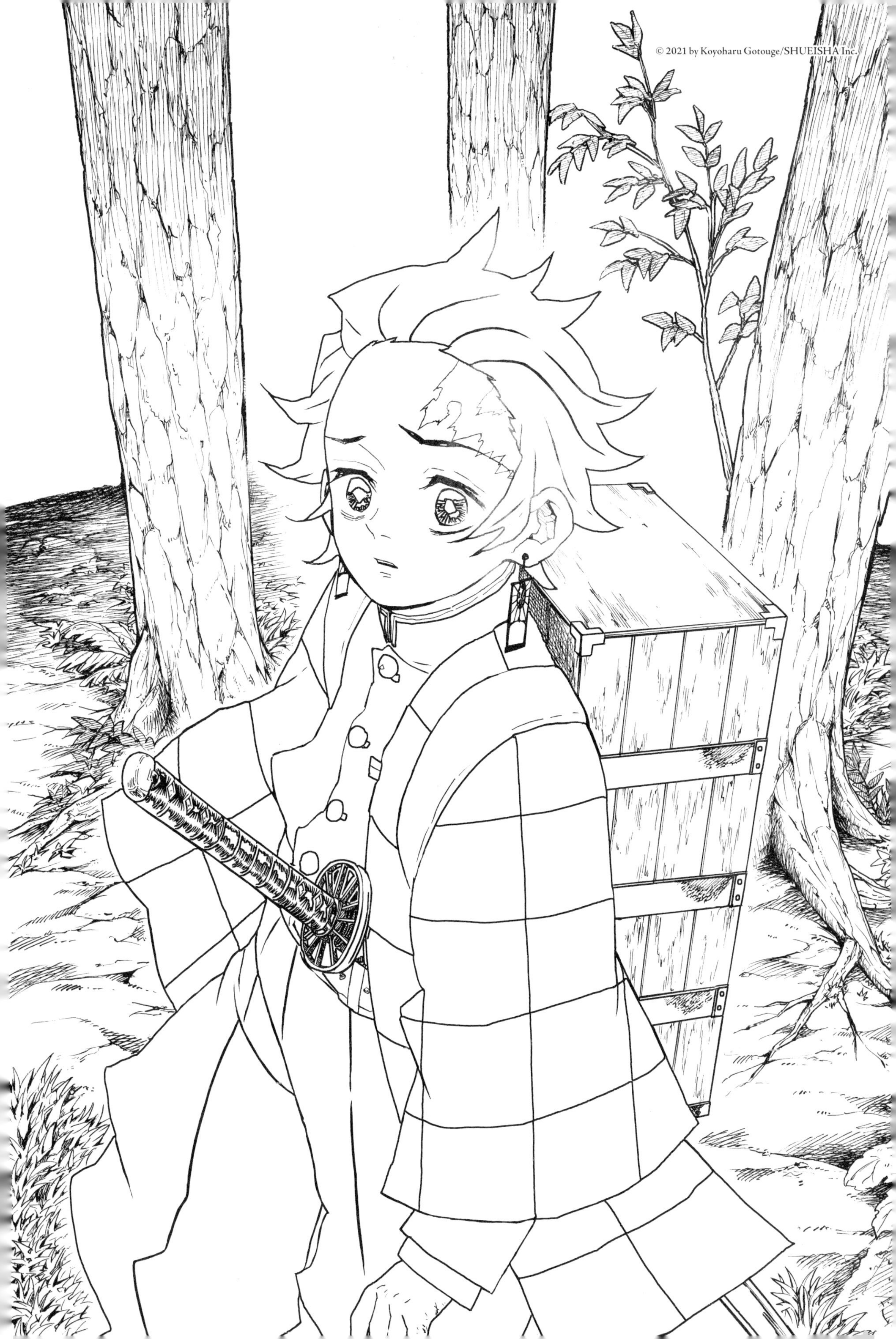

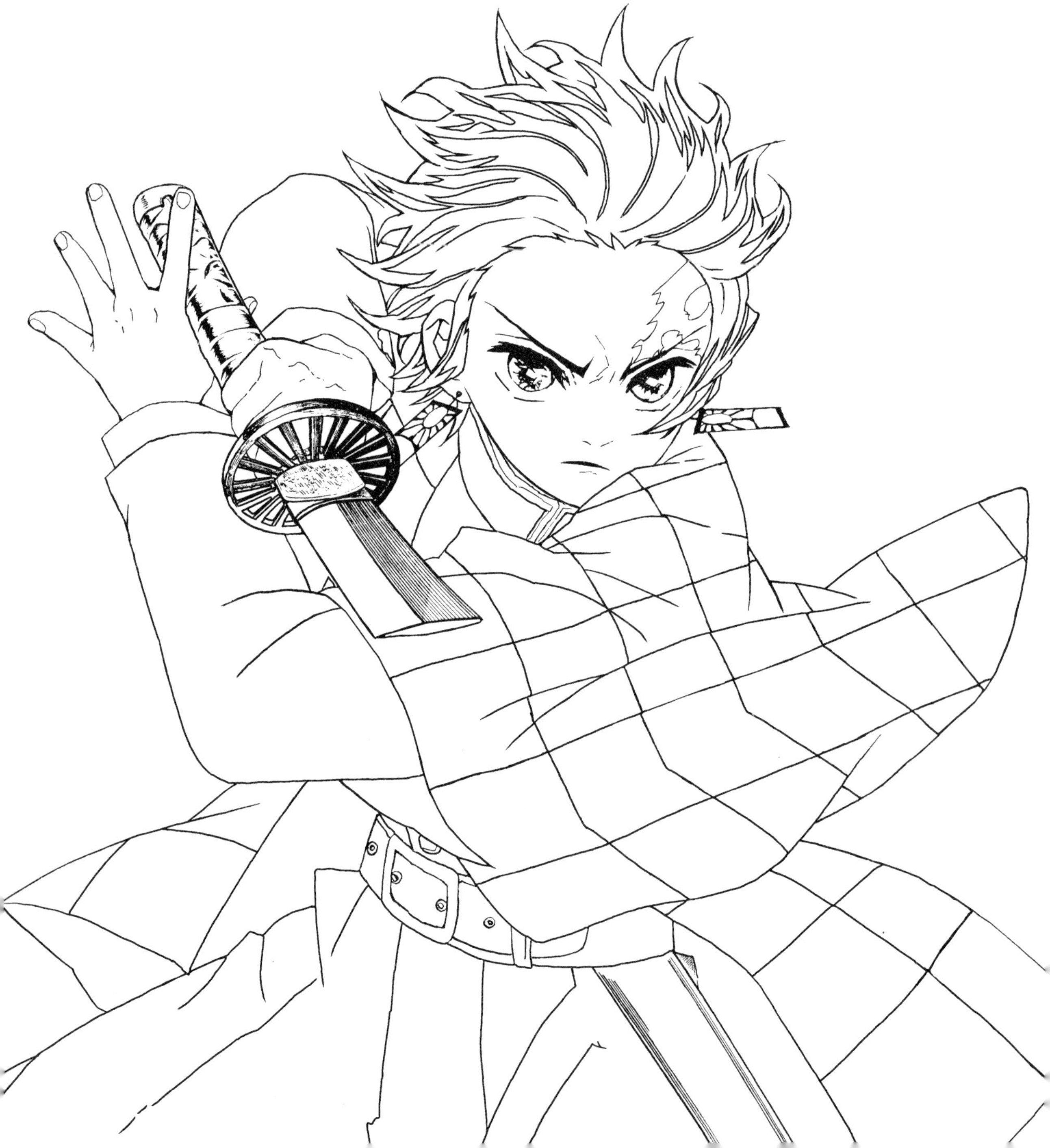

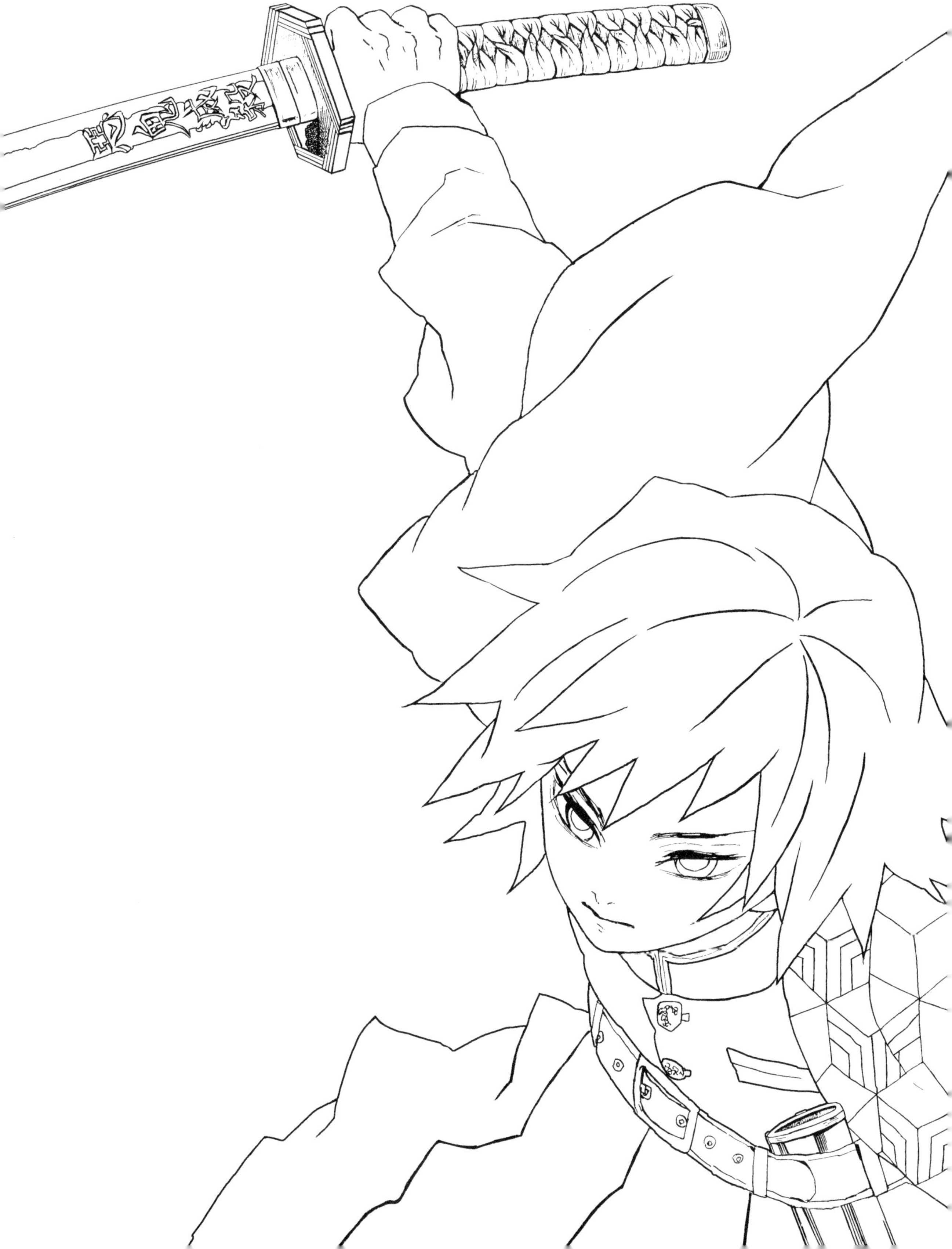

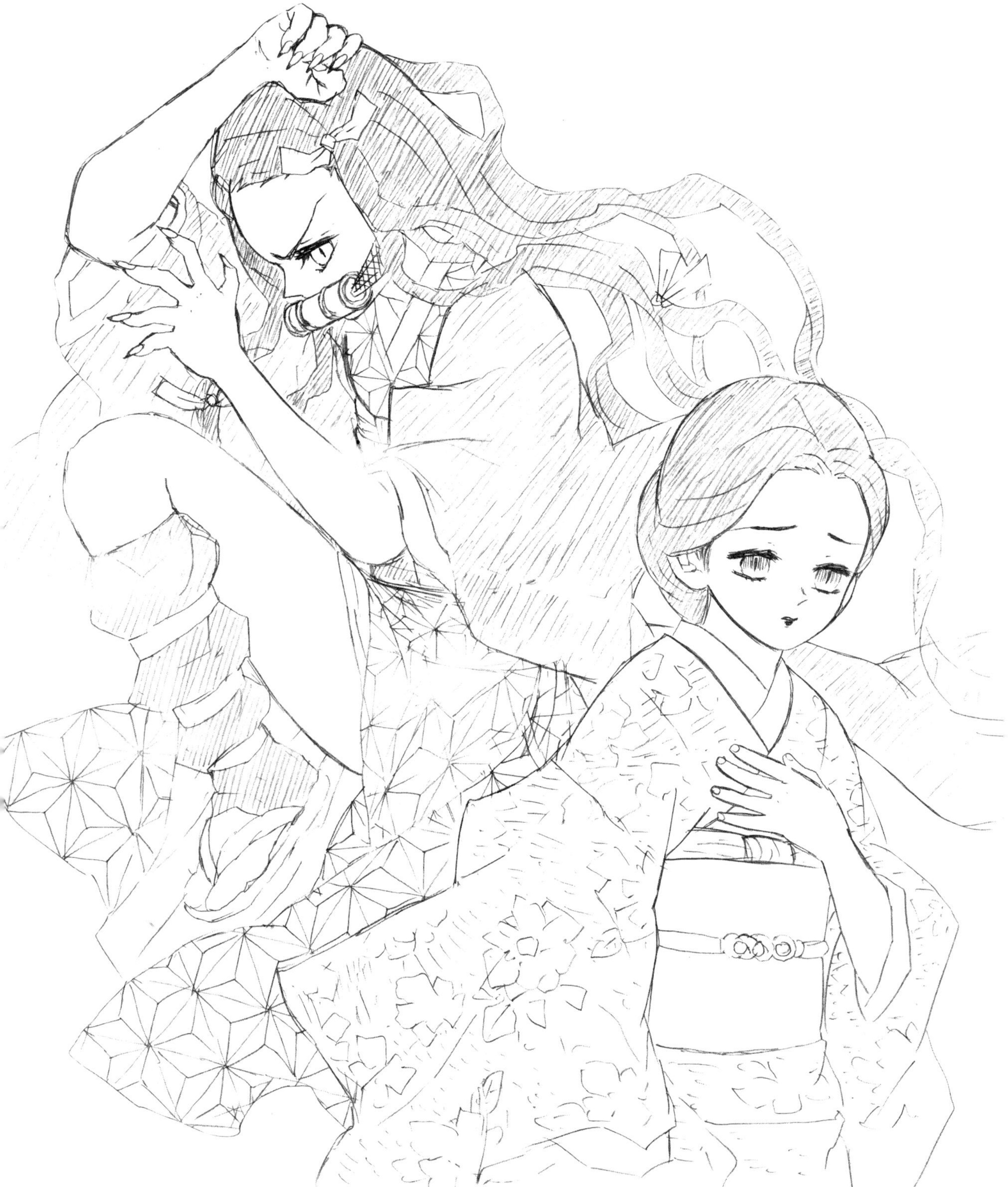

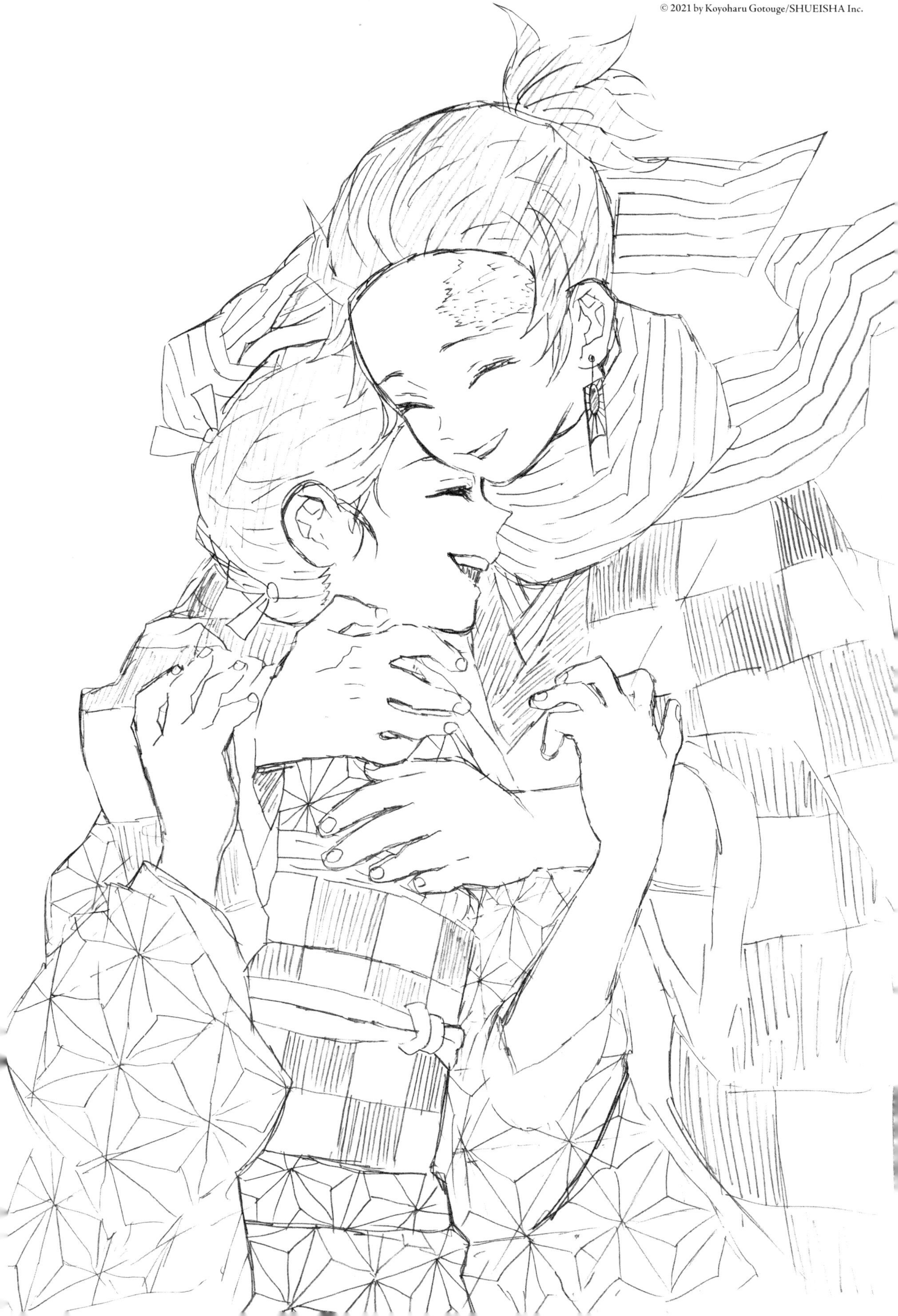

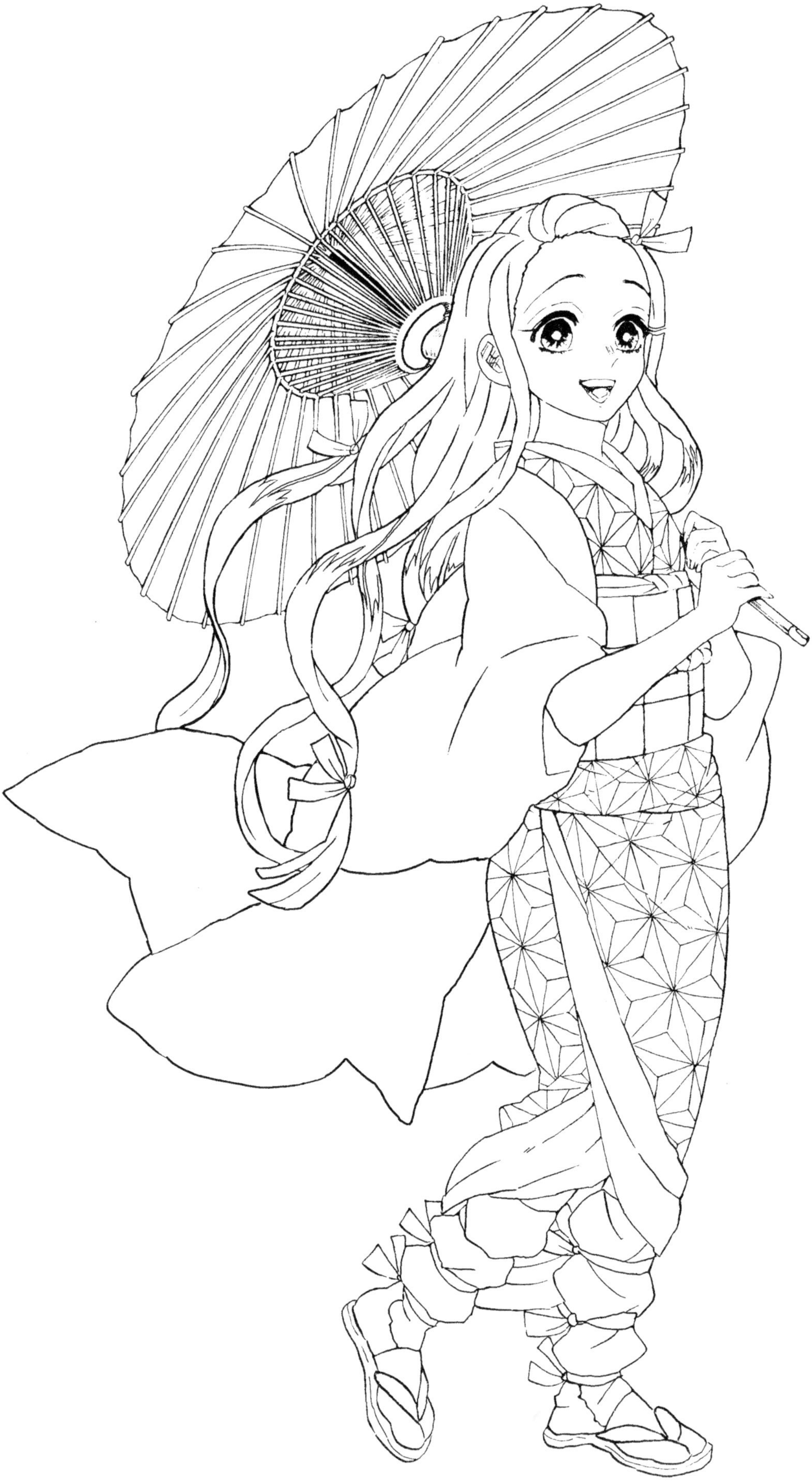

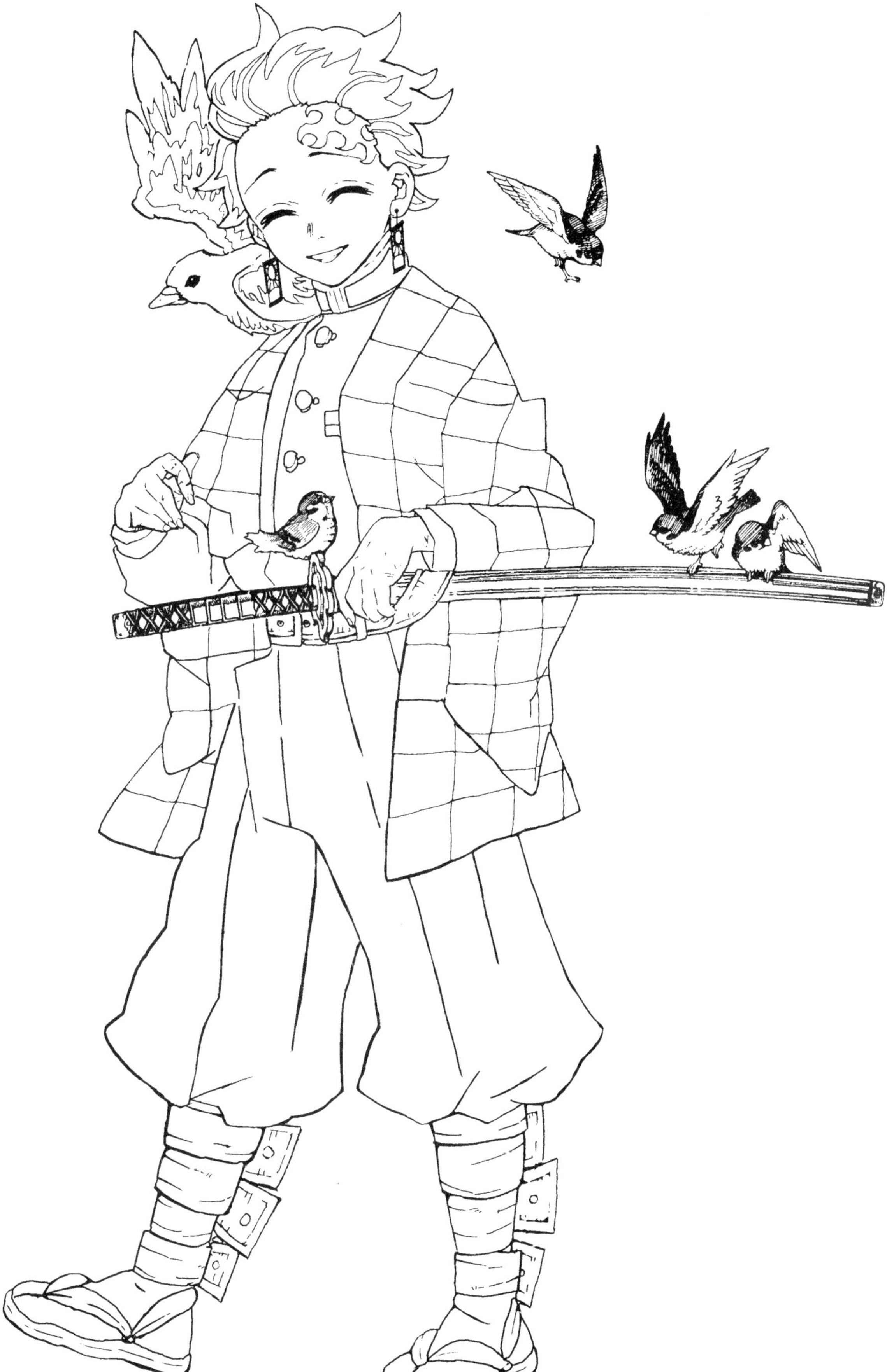

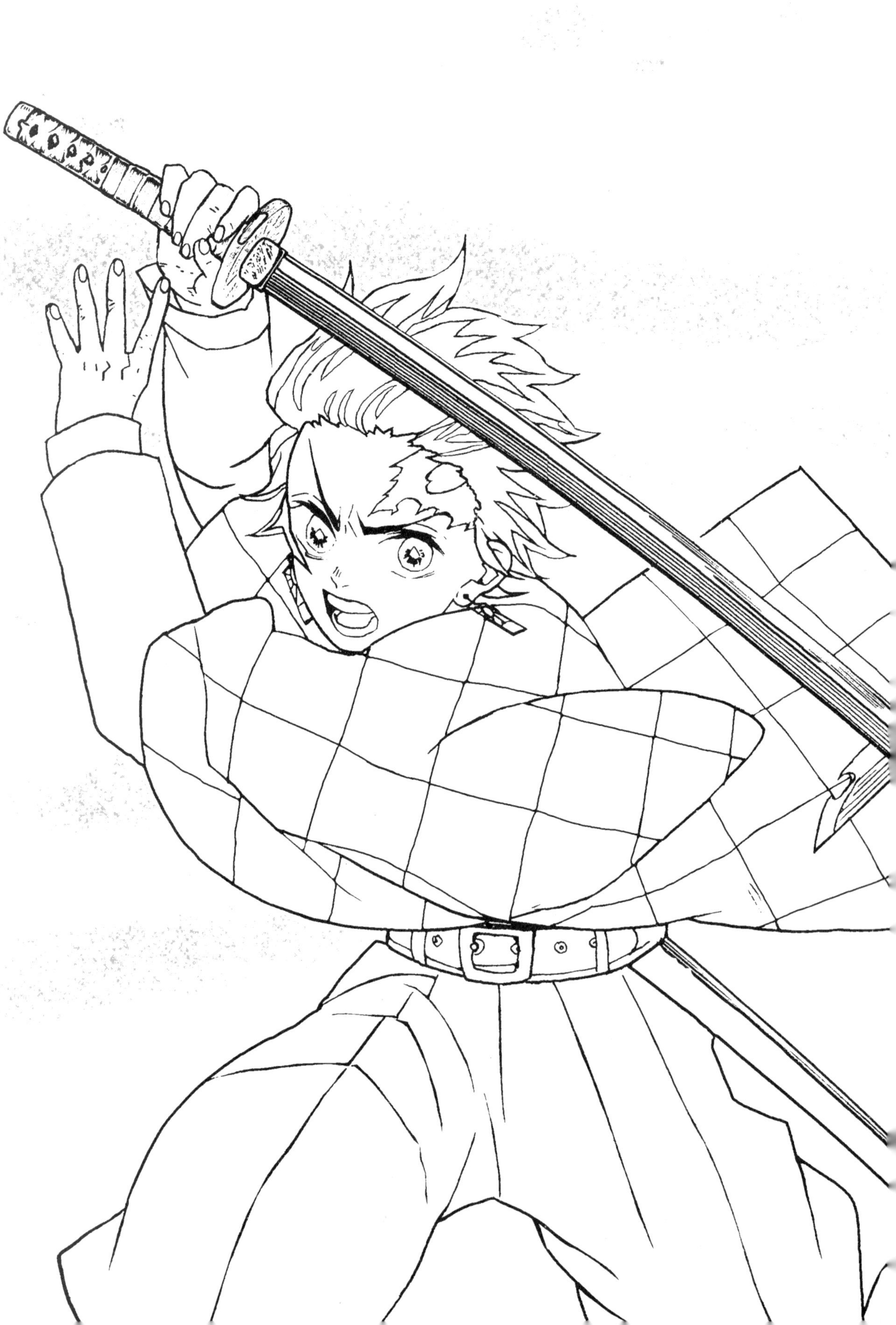

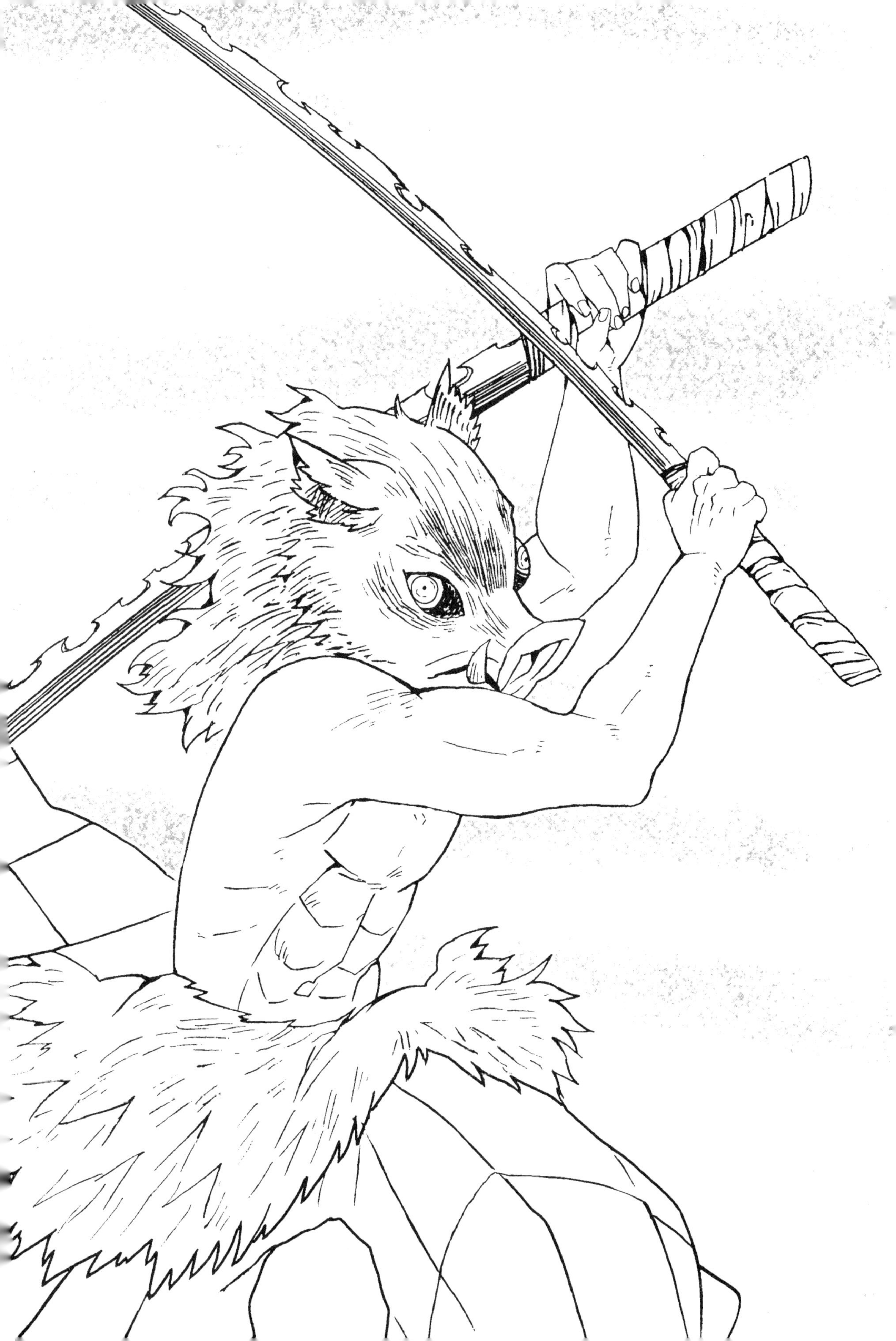

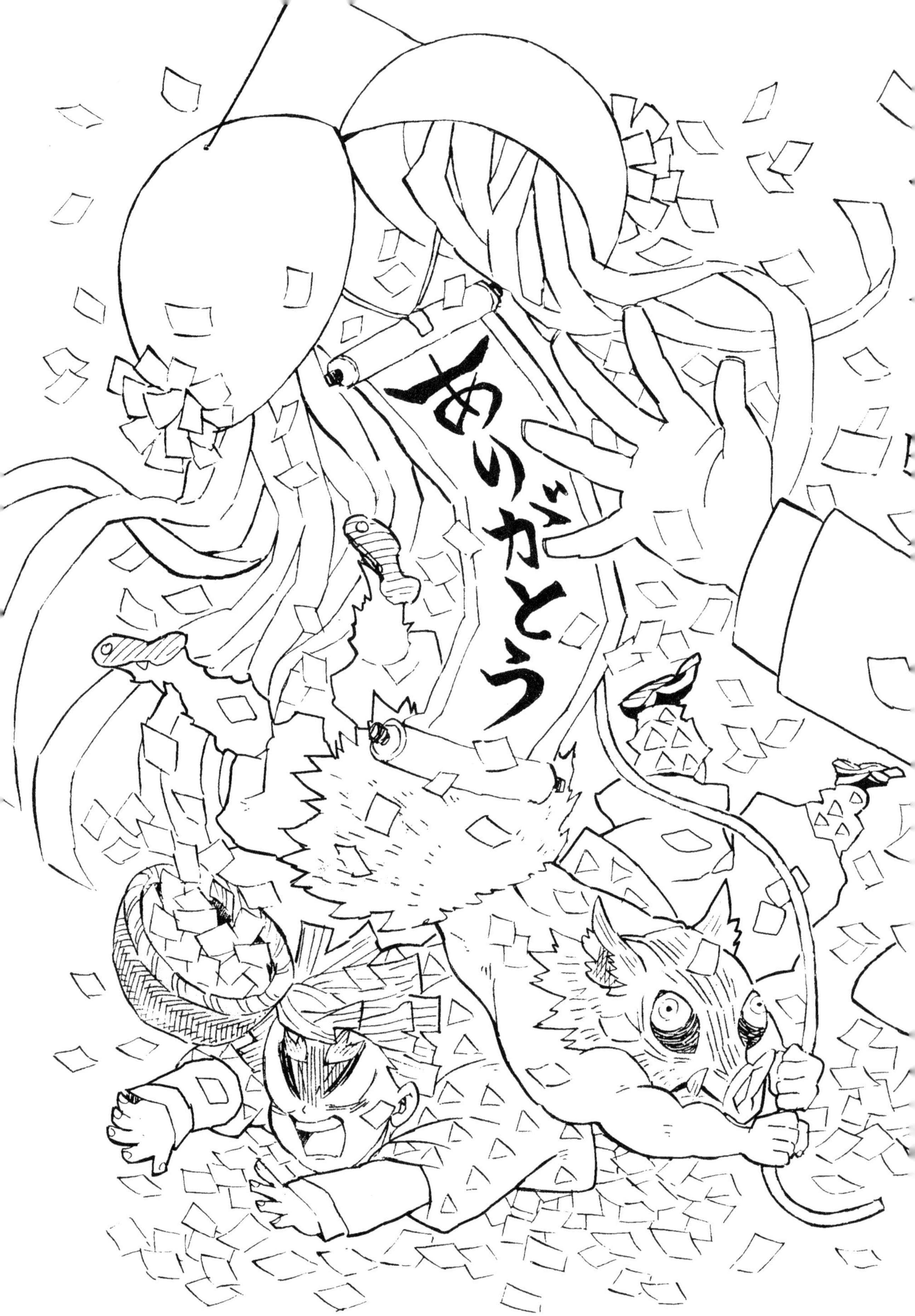
ありがとう

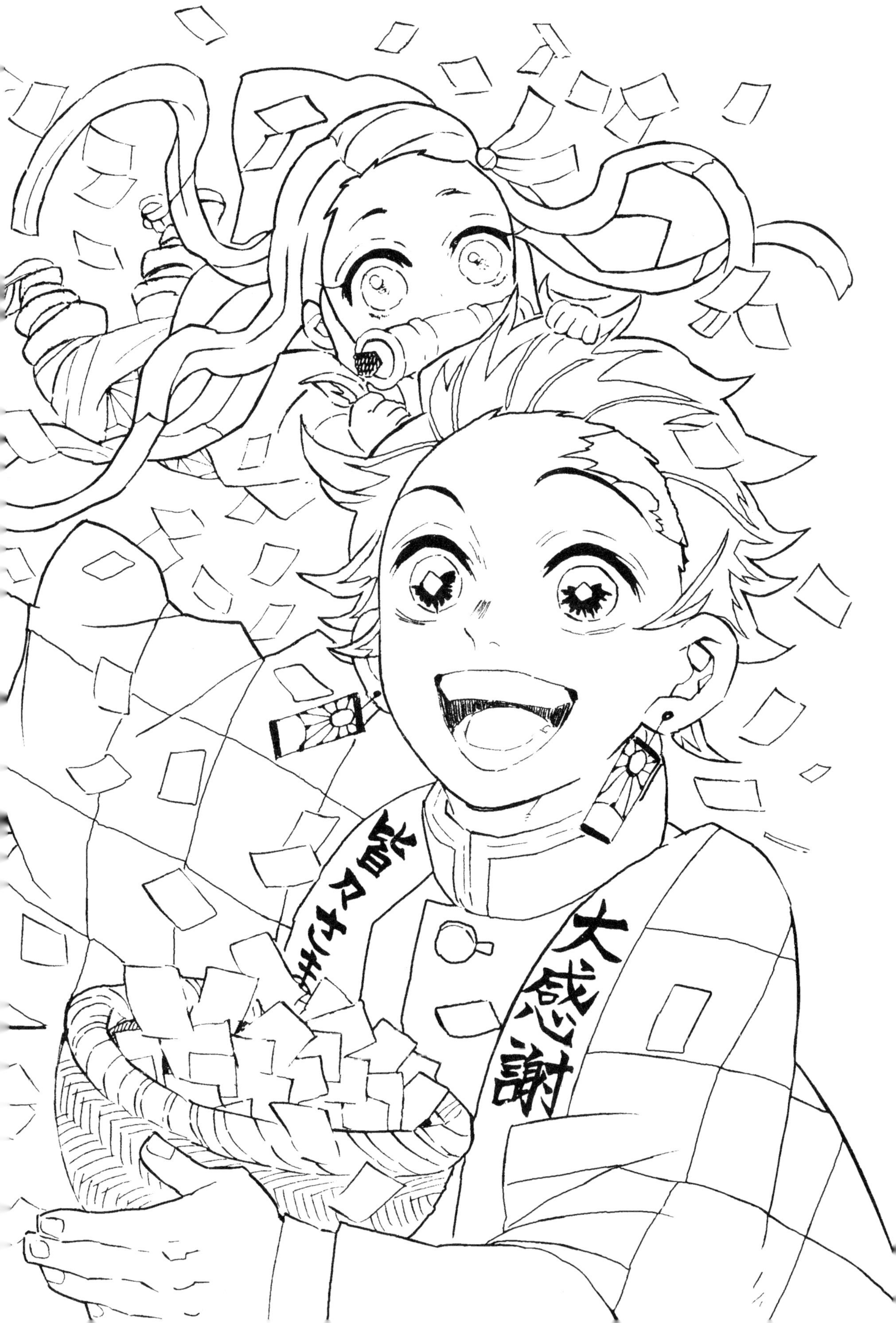
大感謝
皆々さま

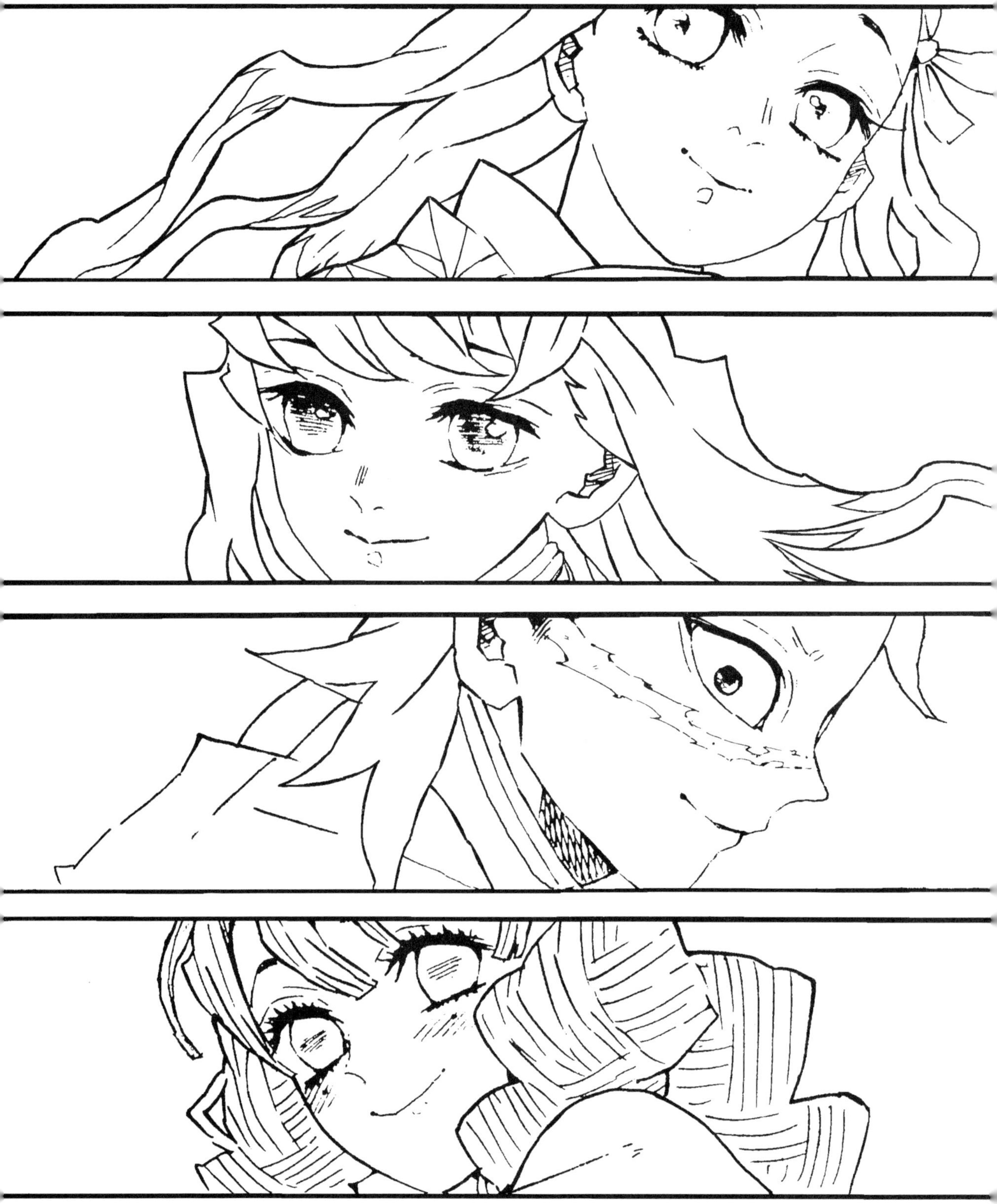

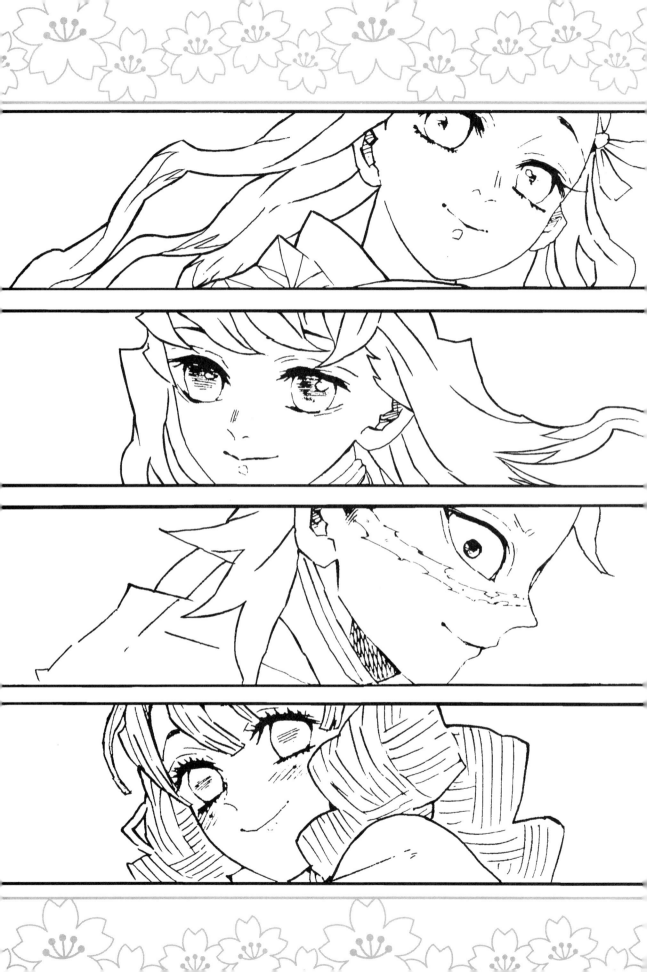

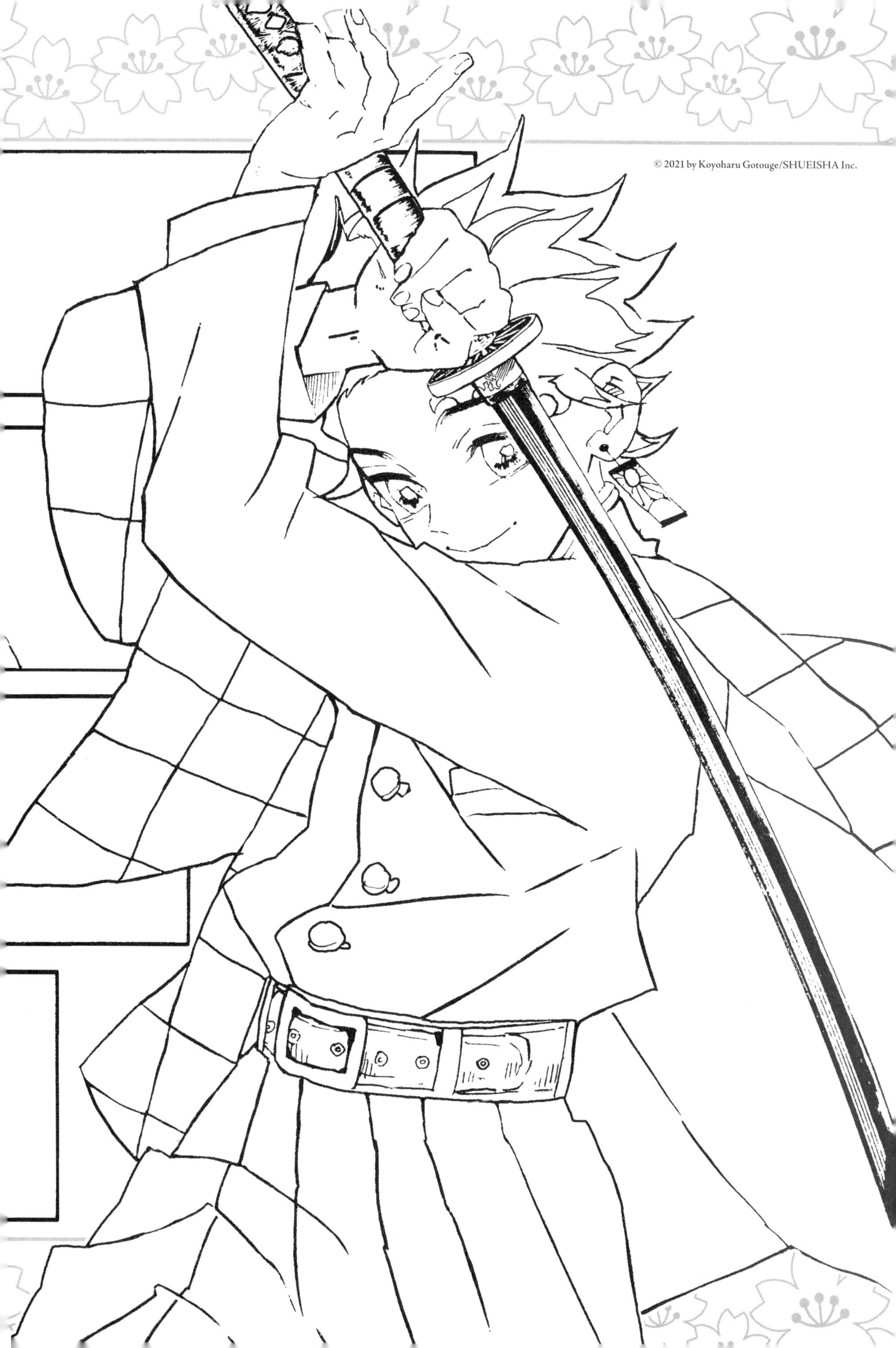

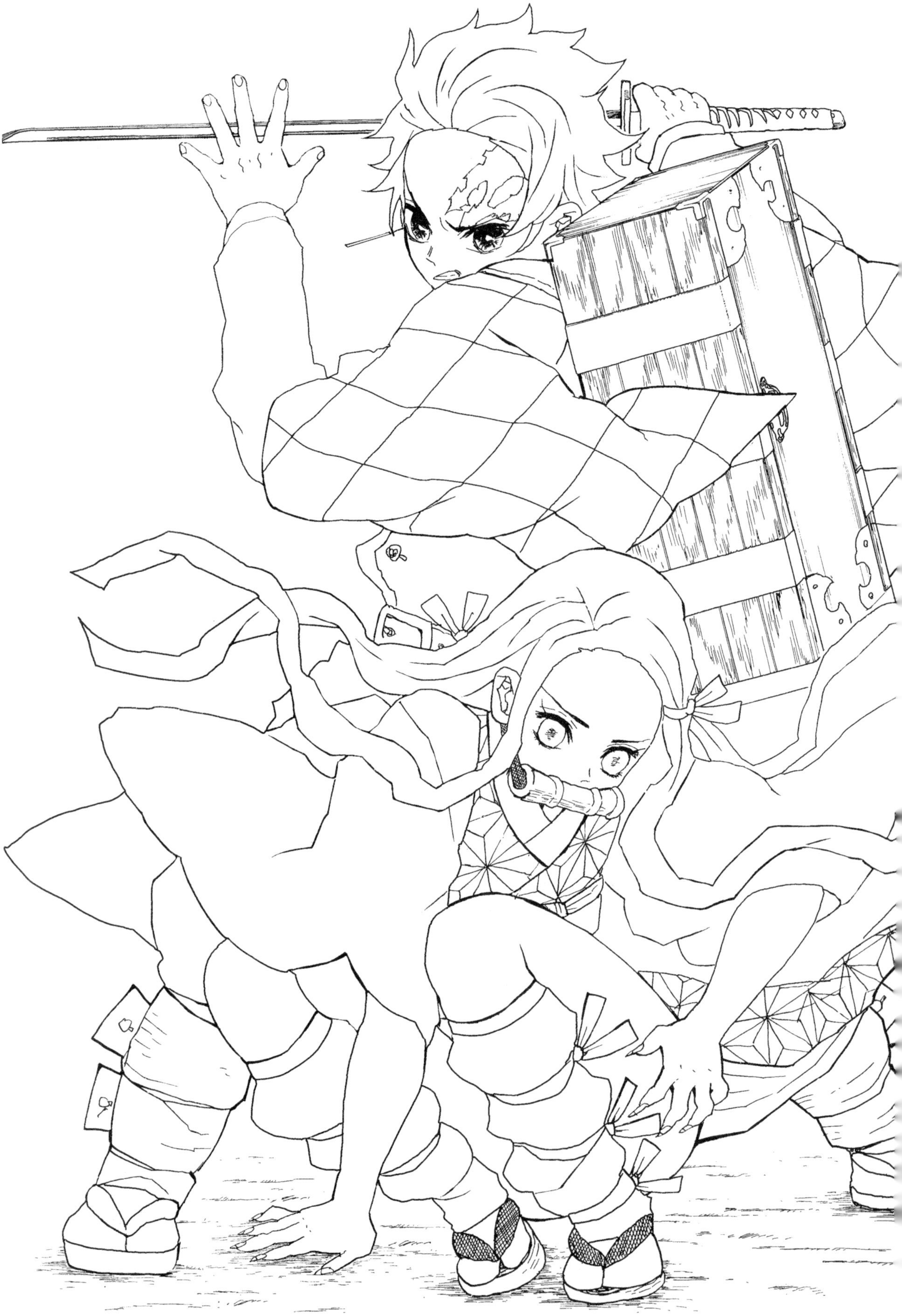

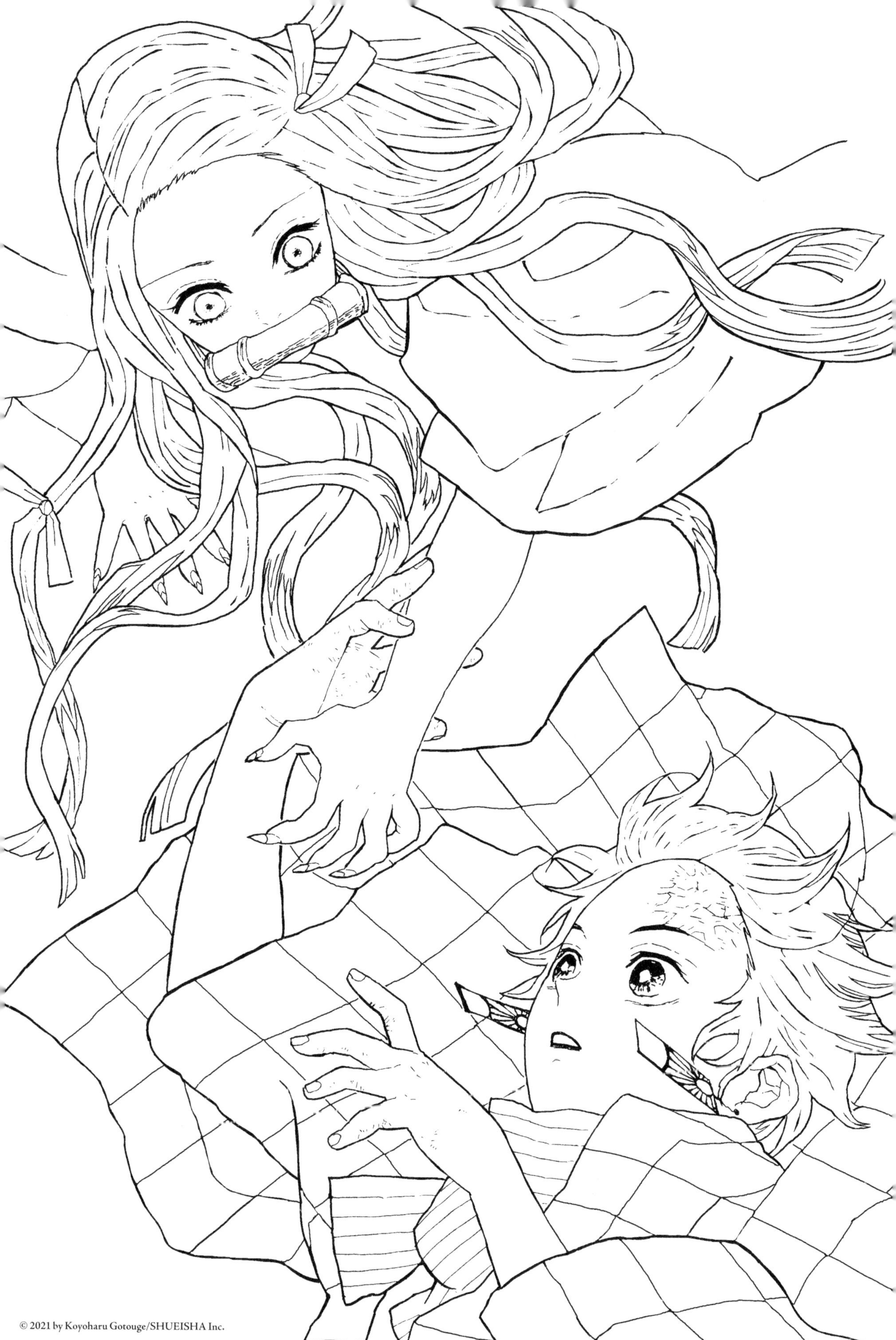

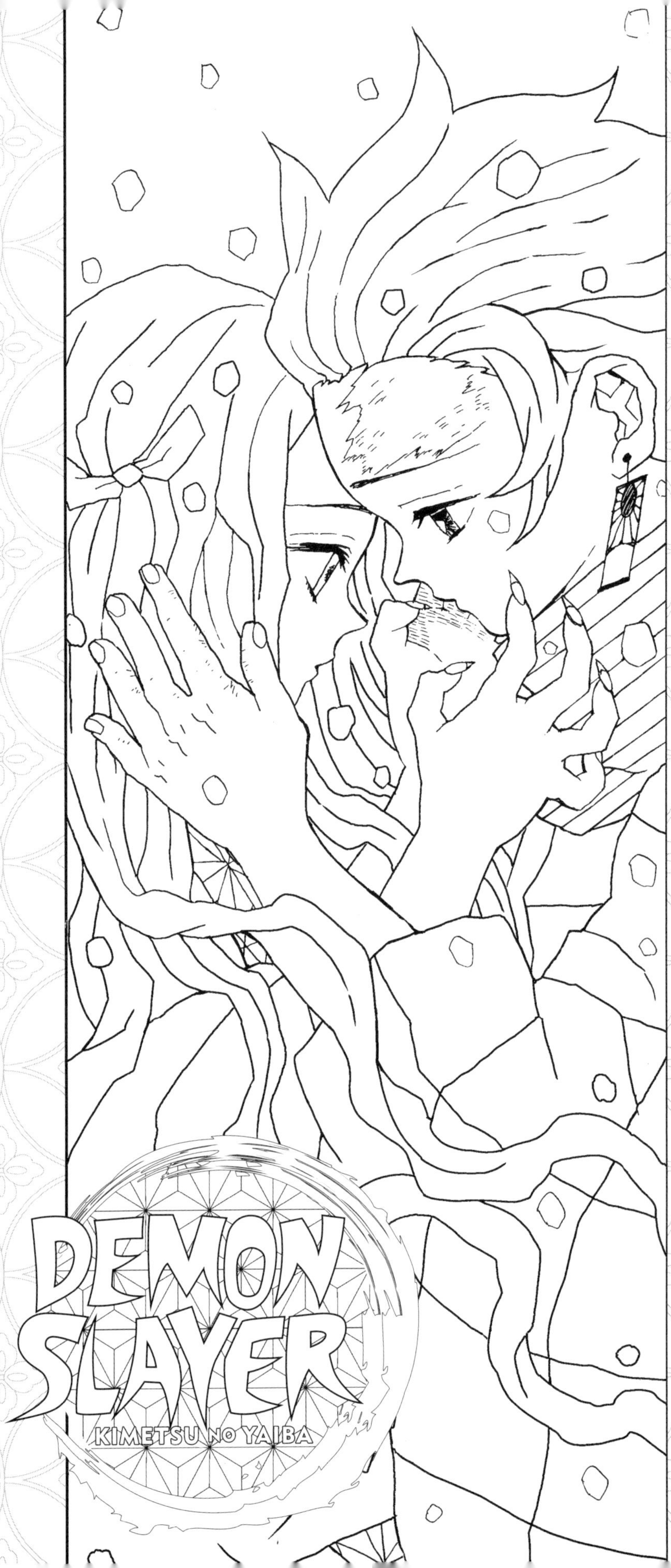
DEMON SLAYER
KIMETSU NO YAIBA

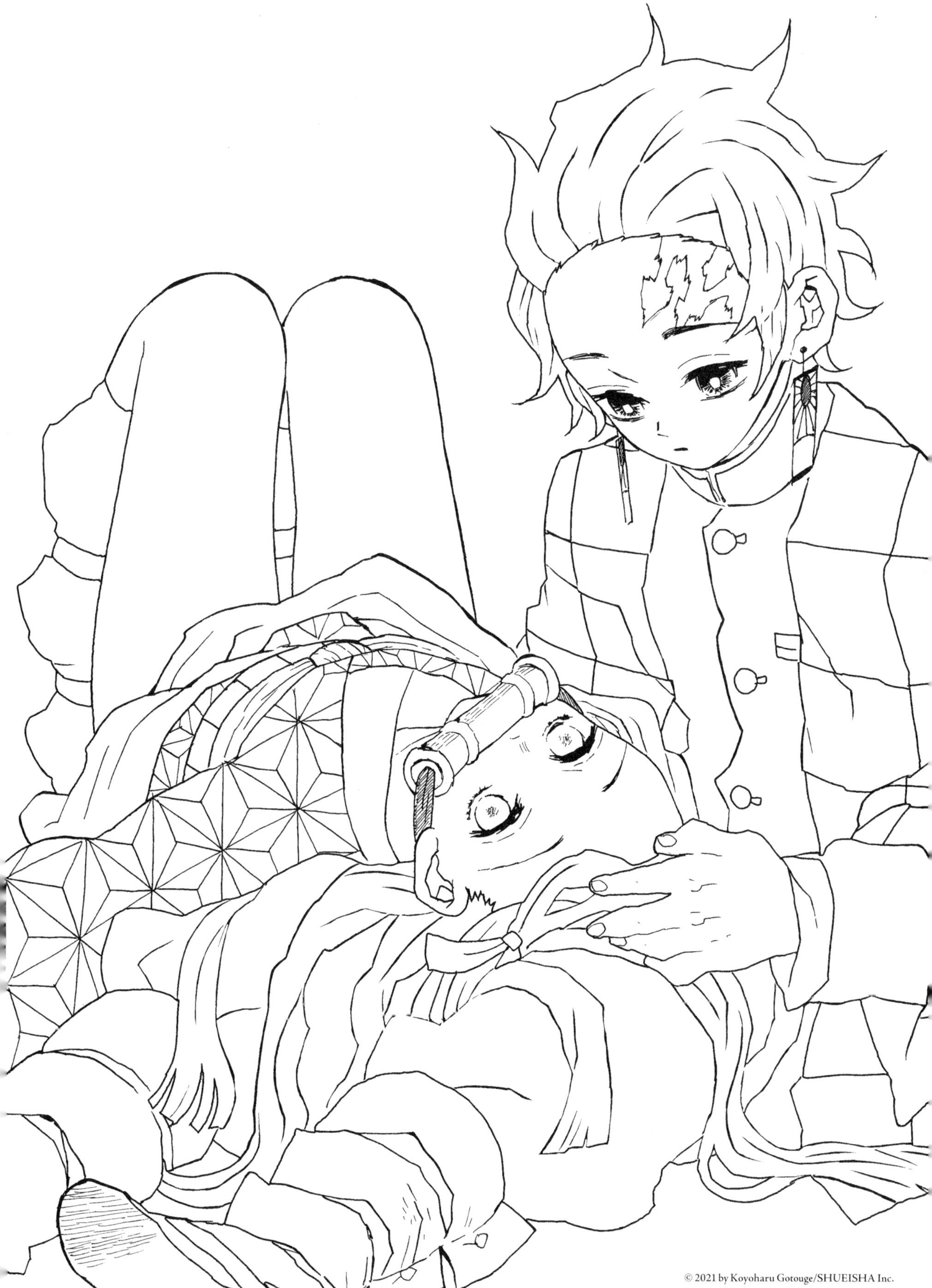

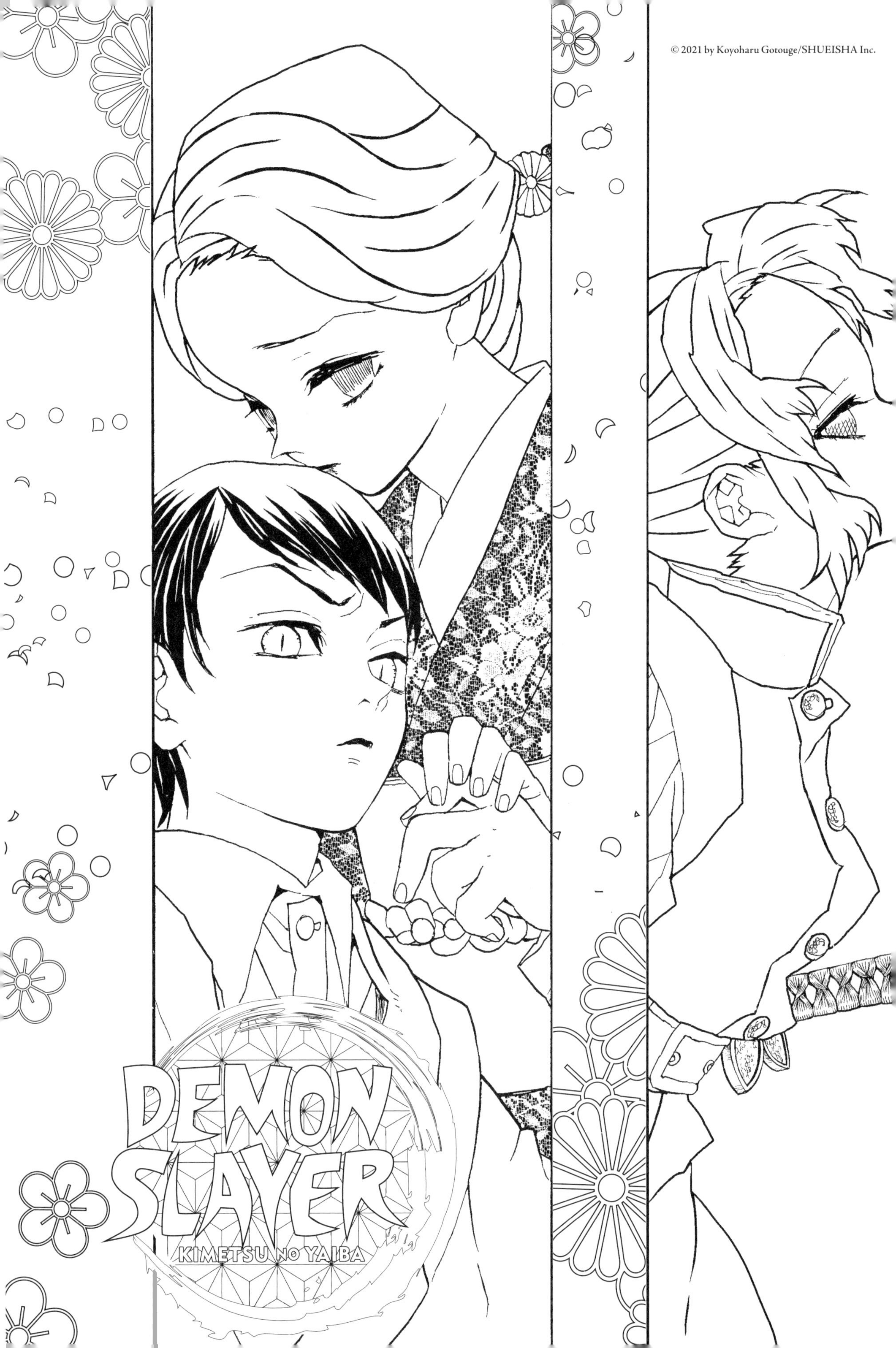
DEMON SLAYER
KIMETSU NO YAIBA

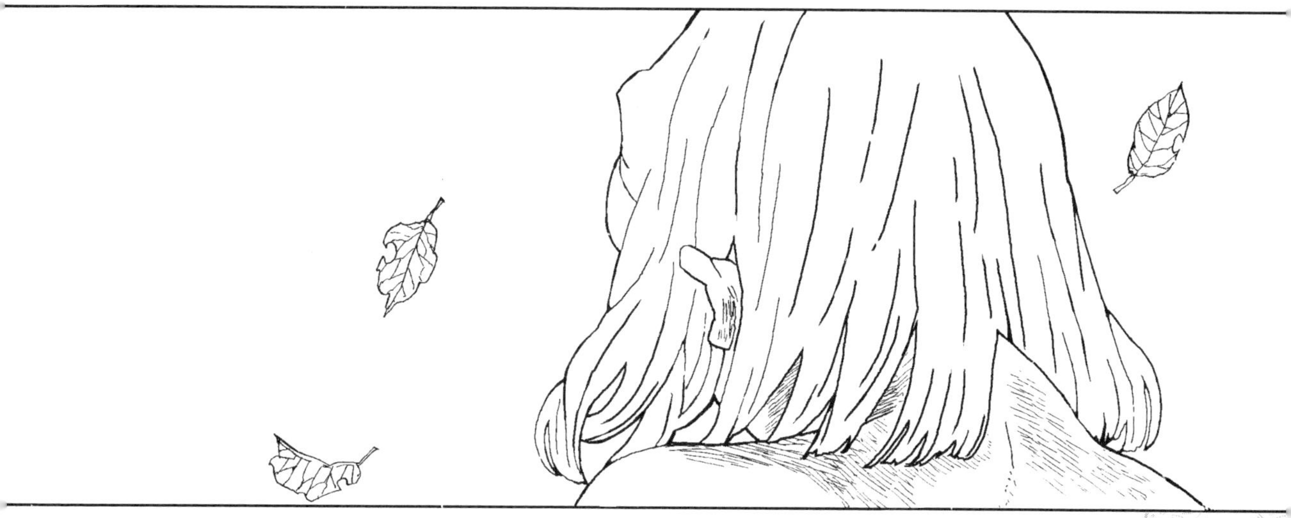

DEMON SLAYER
KIMETSU NO YAIBA

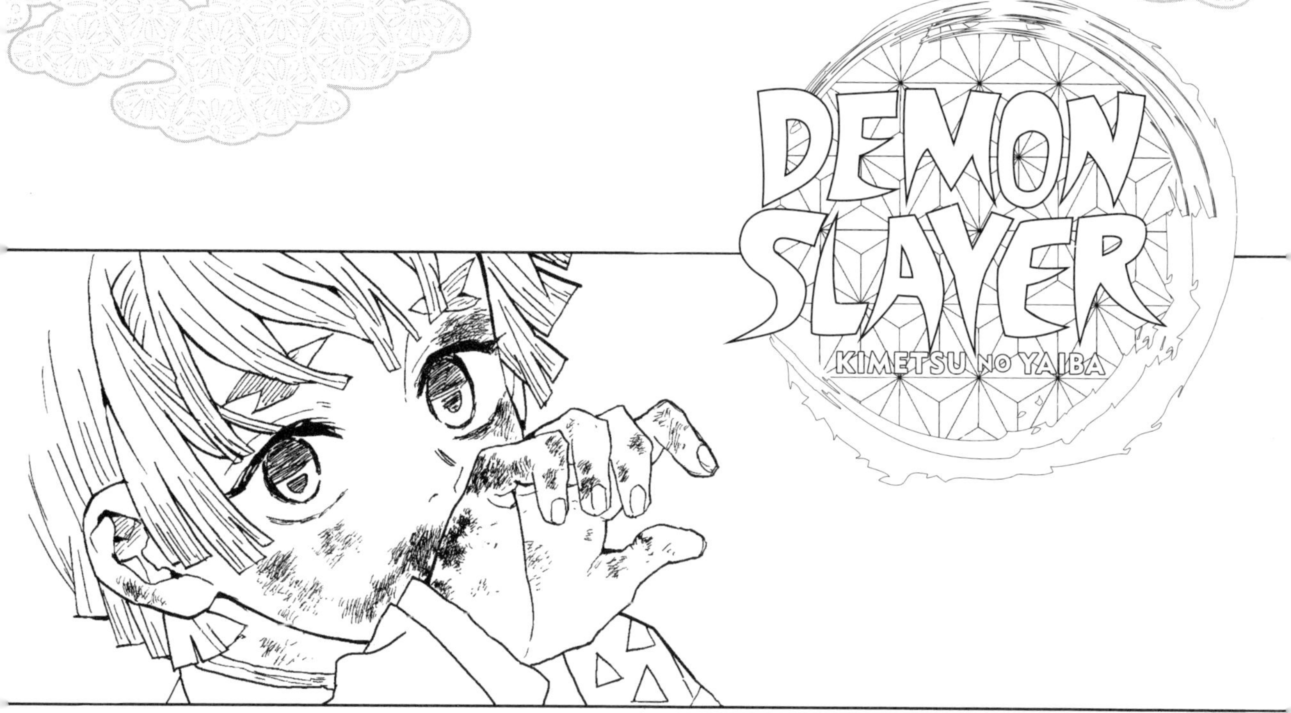

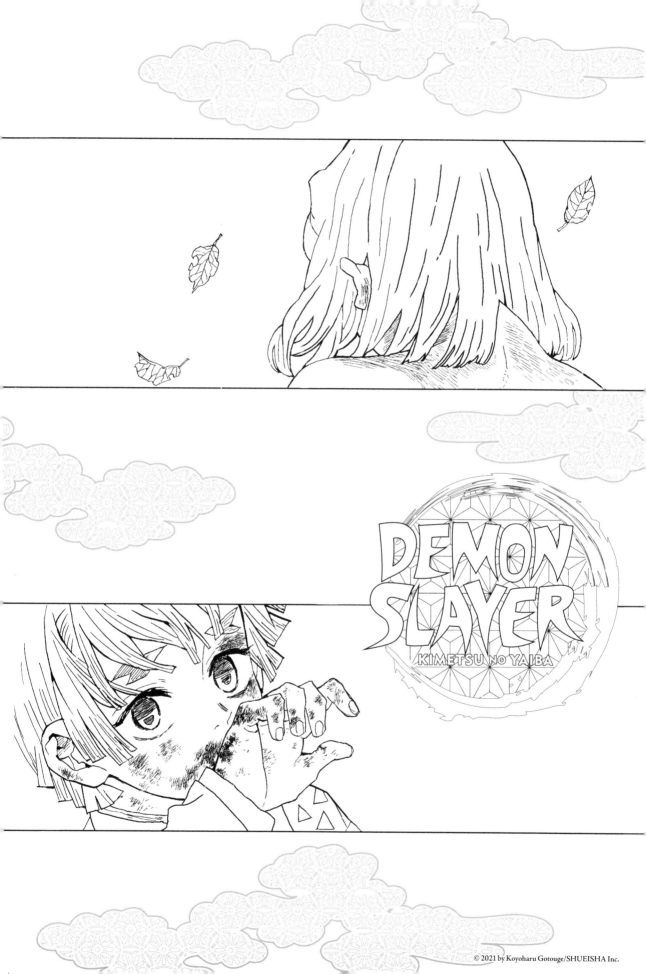

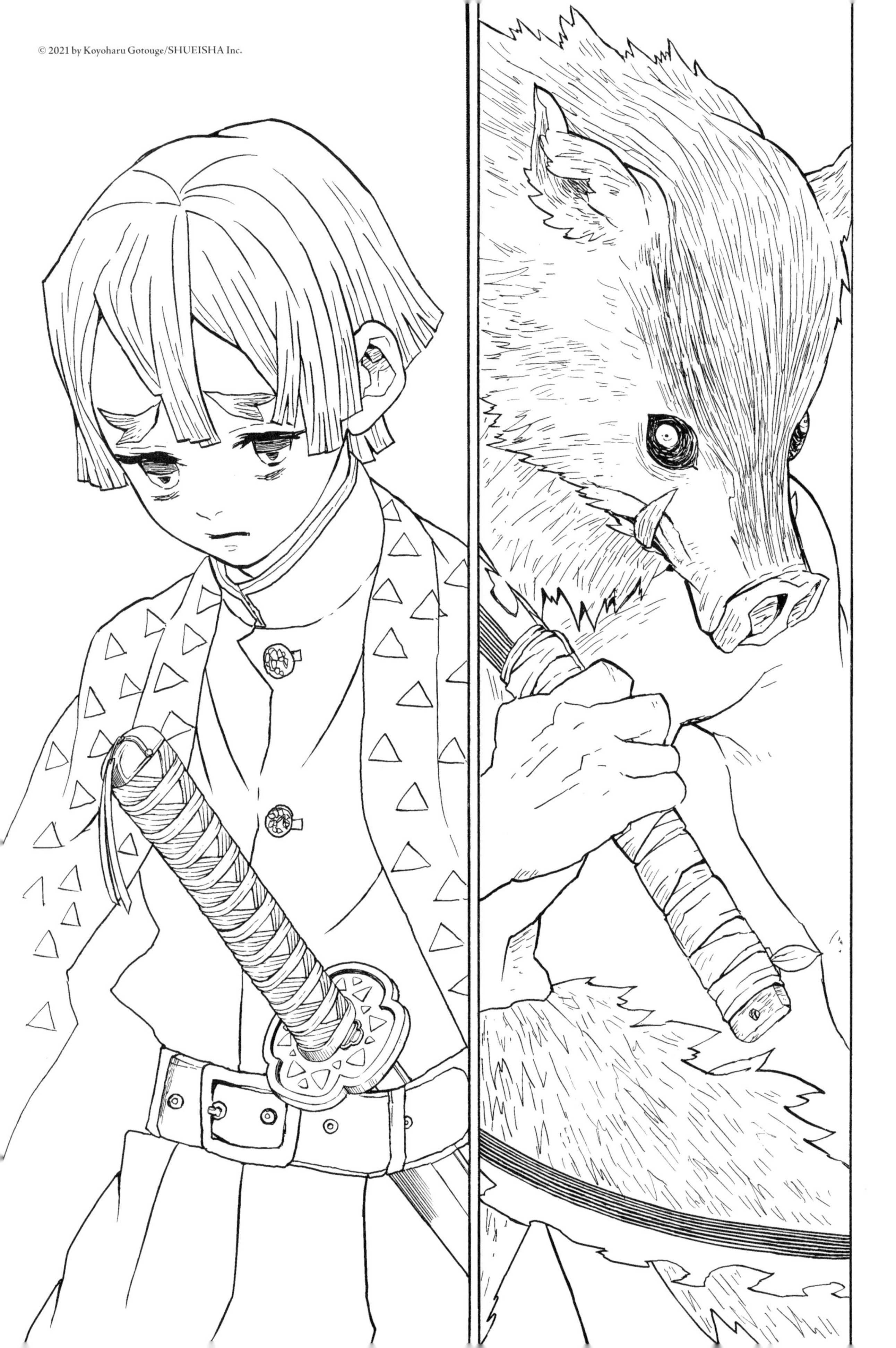

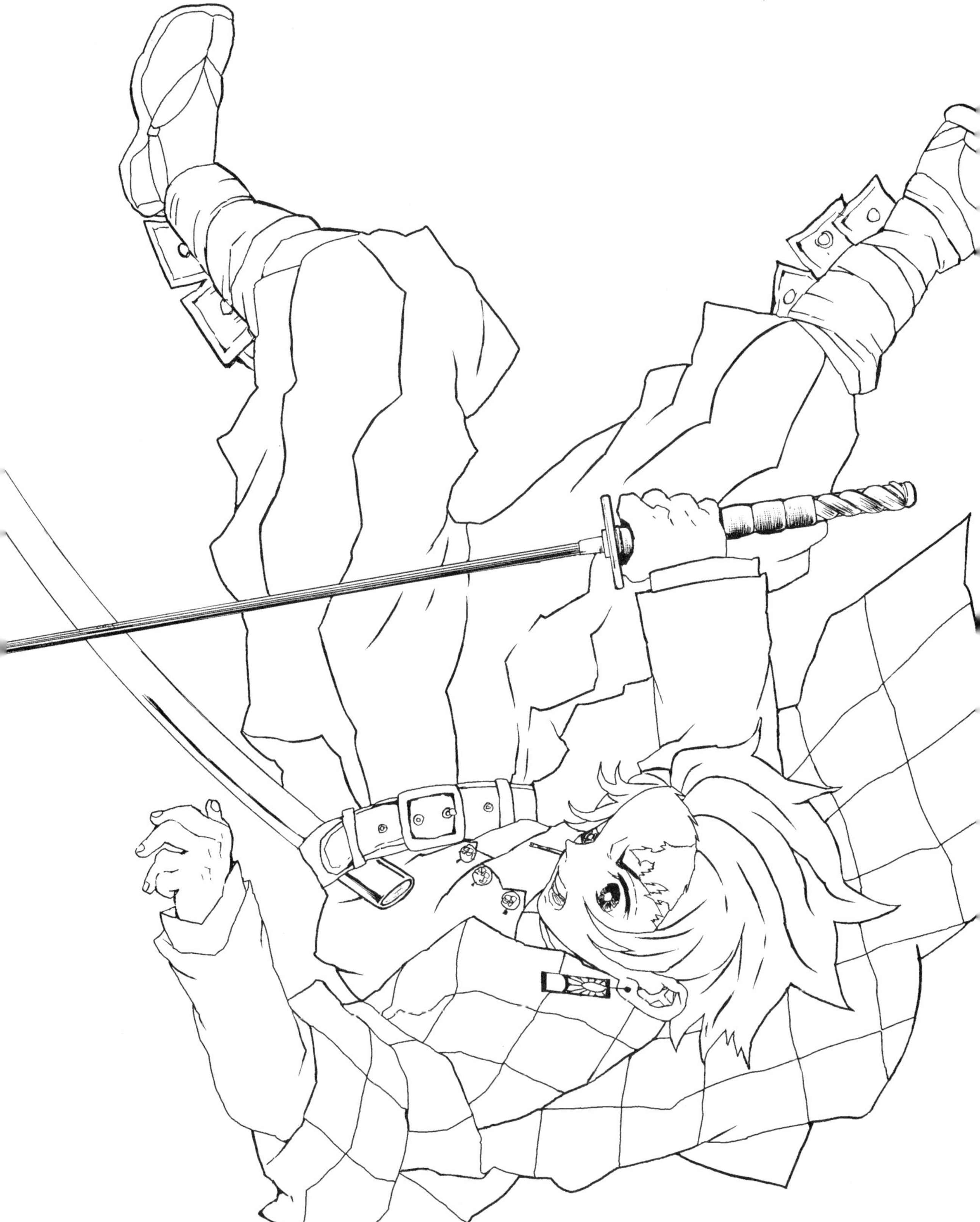

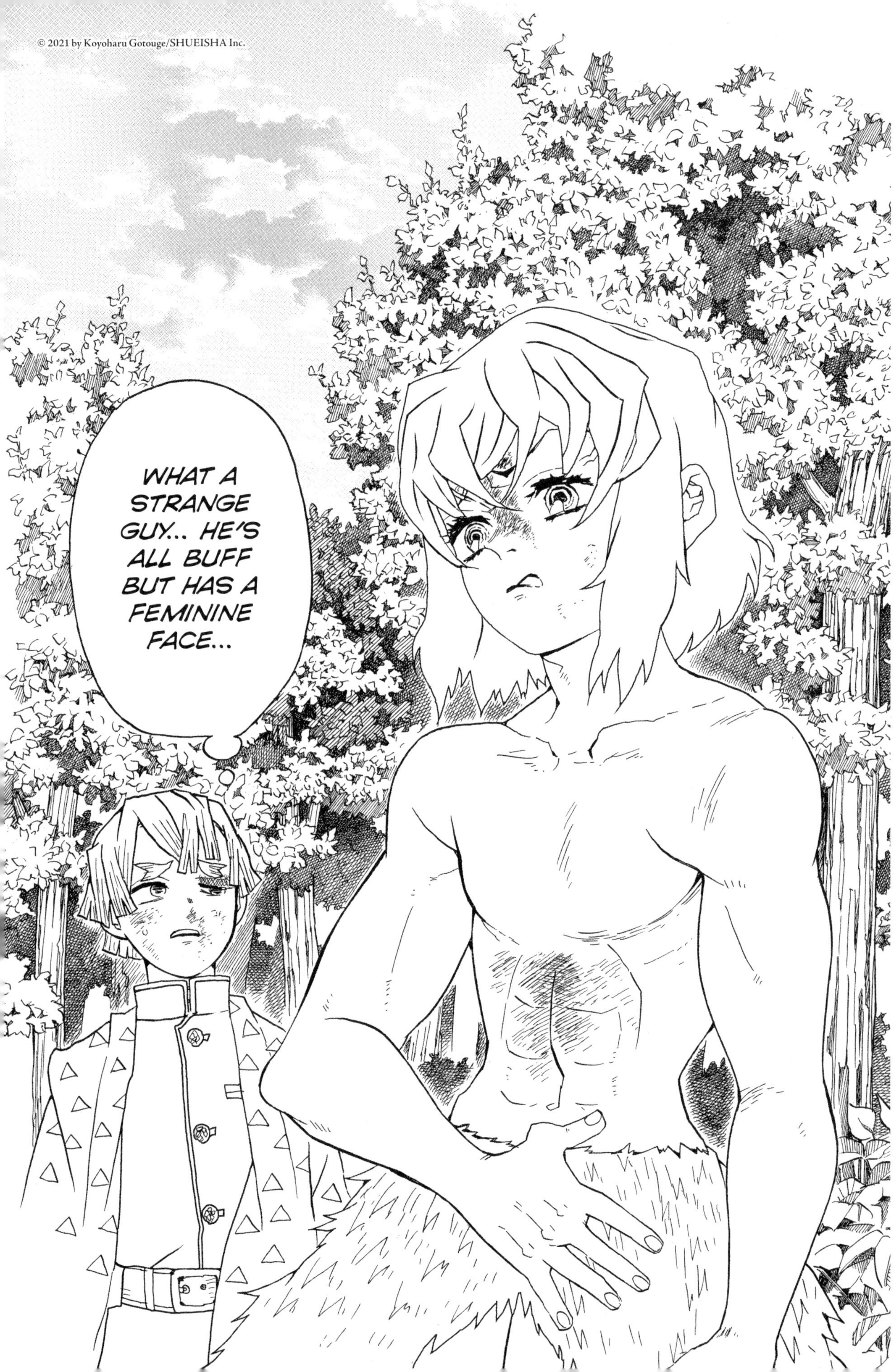
WHAT A STRANGE GUY... HE'S ALL BUFF BUT HAS A FEMININE FACE...

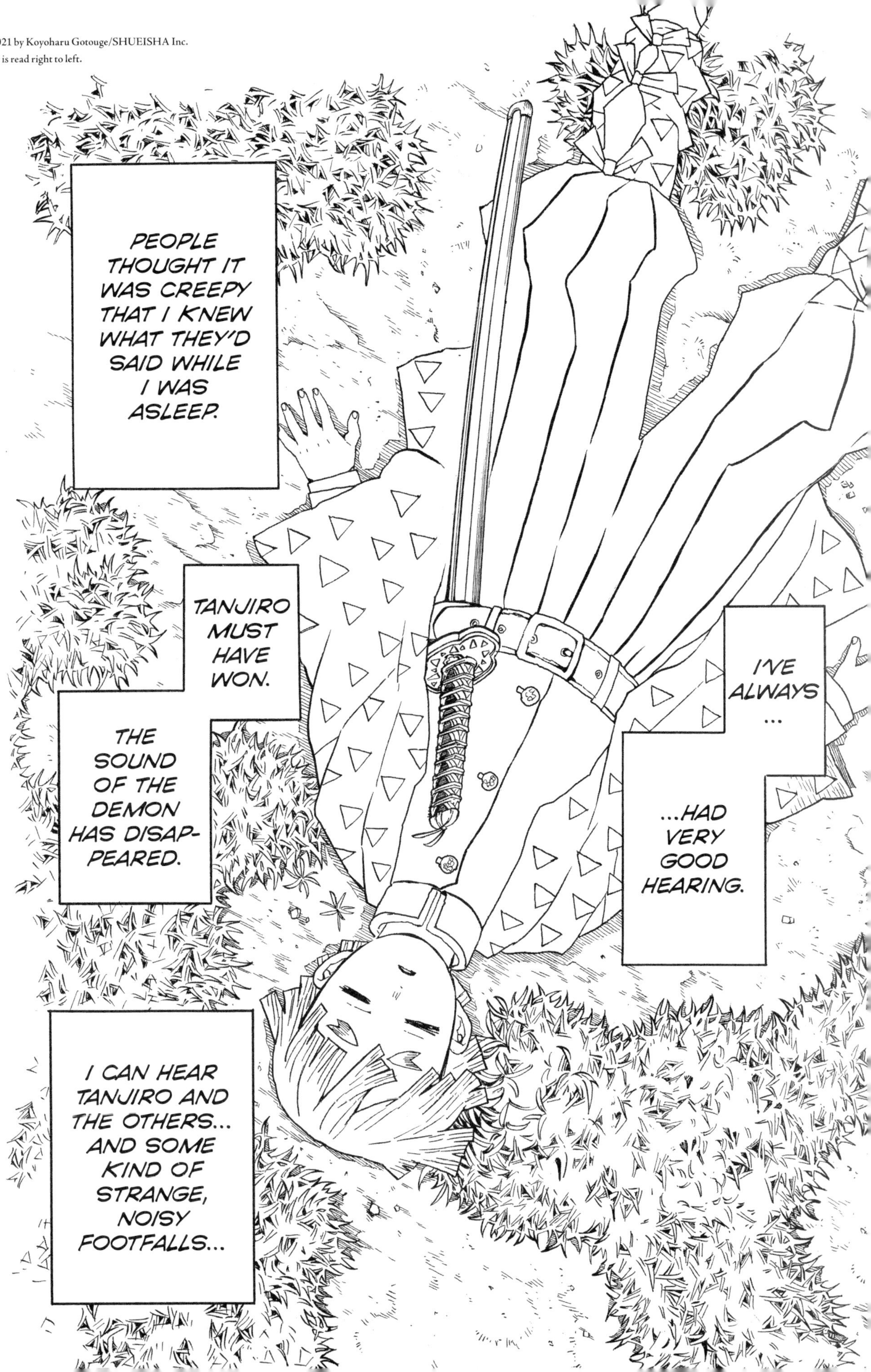
I'VE ALWAYS...
...HAD VERY GOOD HEARING.
PEOPLE THOUGHT IT WAS CREEPY THAT I KNEW WHAT THEY'D SAID WHILE I WAS ASLEEP.
TANJIRO MUST HAVE WON.
THE SOUND OF THE DEMON HAS DISAPPEARED.
I CAN HEAR TANJIRO AND THE OTHERS... AND SOME KIND OF STRANGE, NOISY FOOTFALLS...

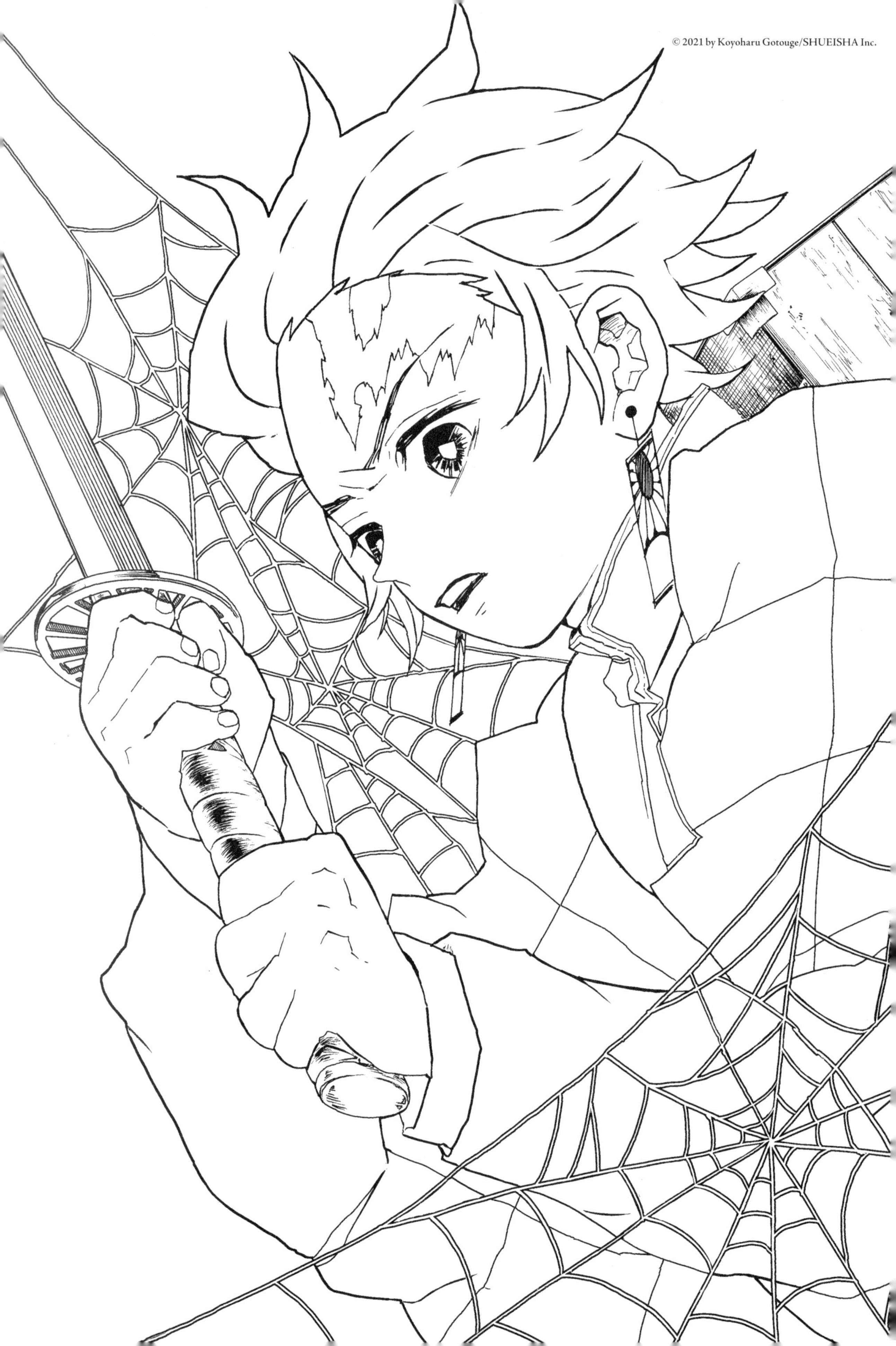

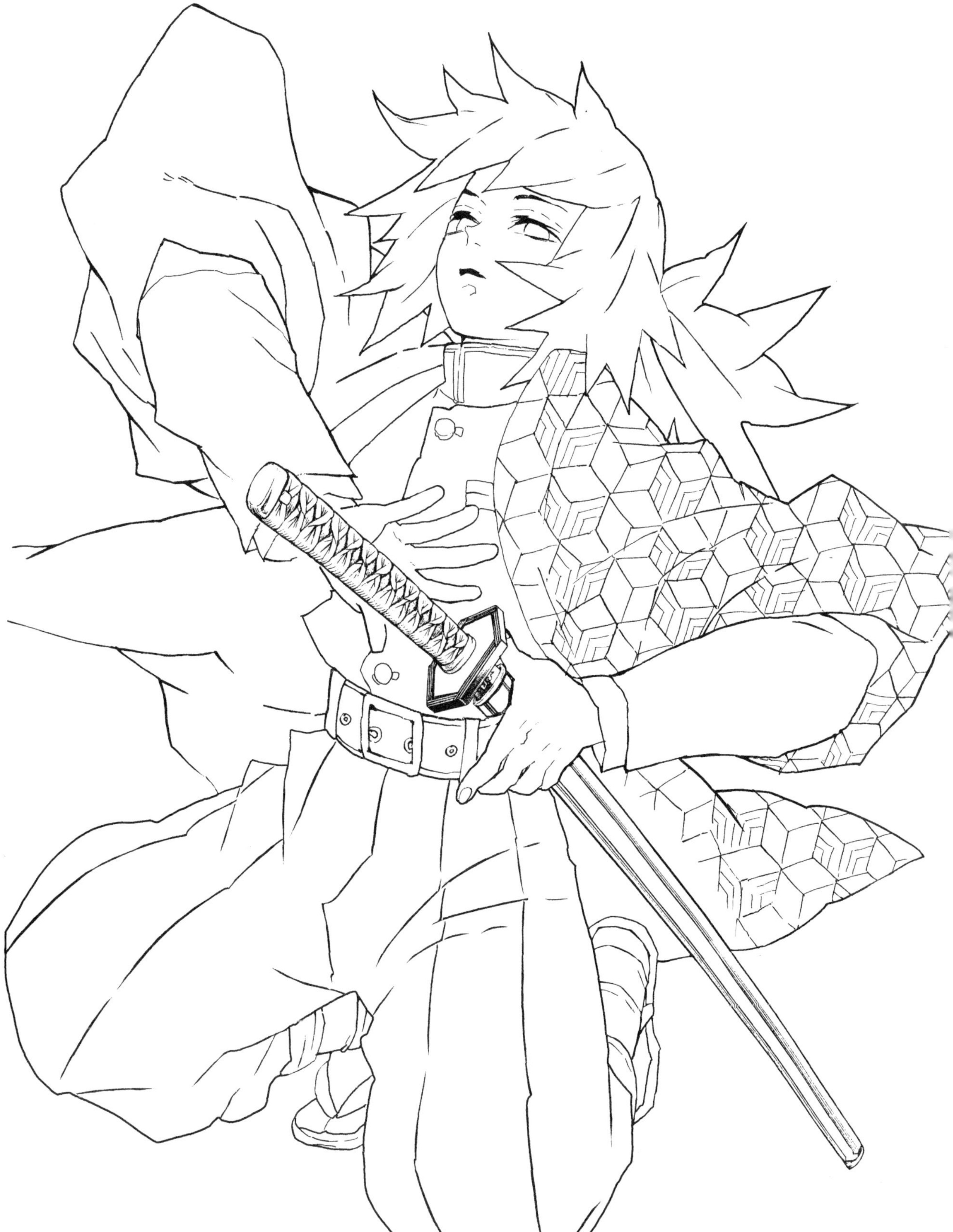

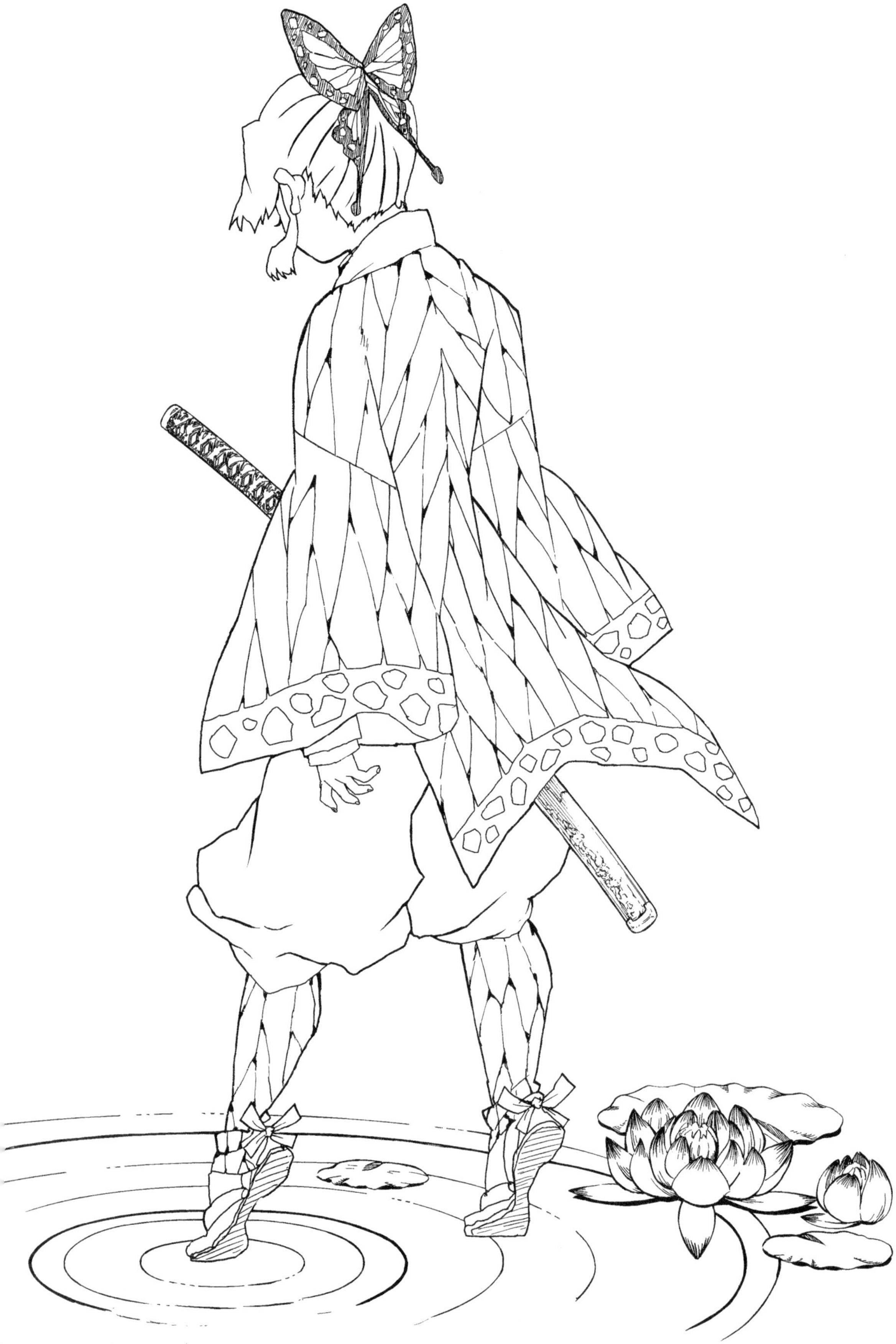

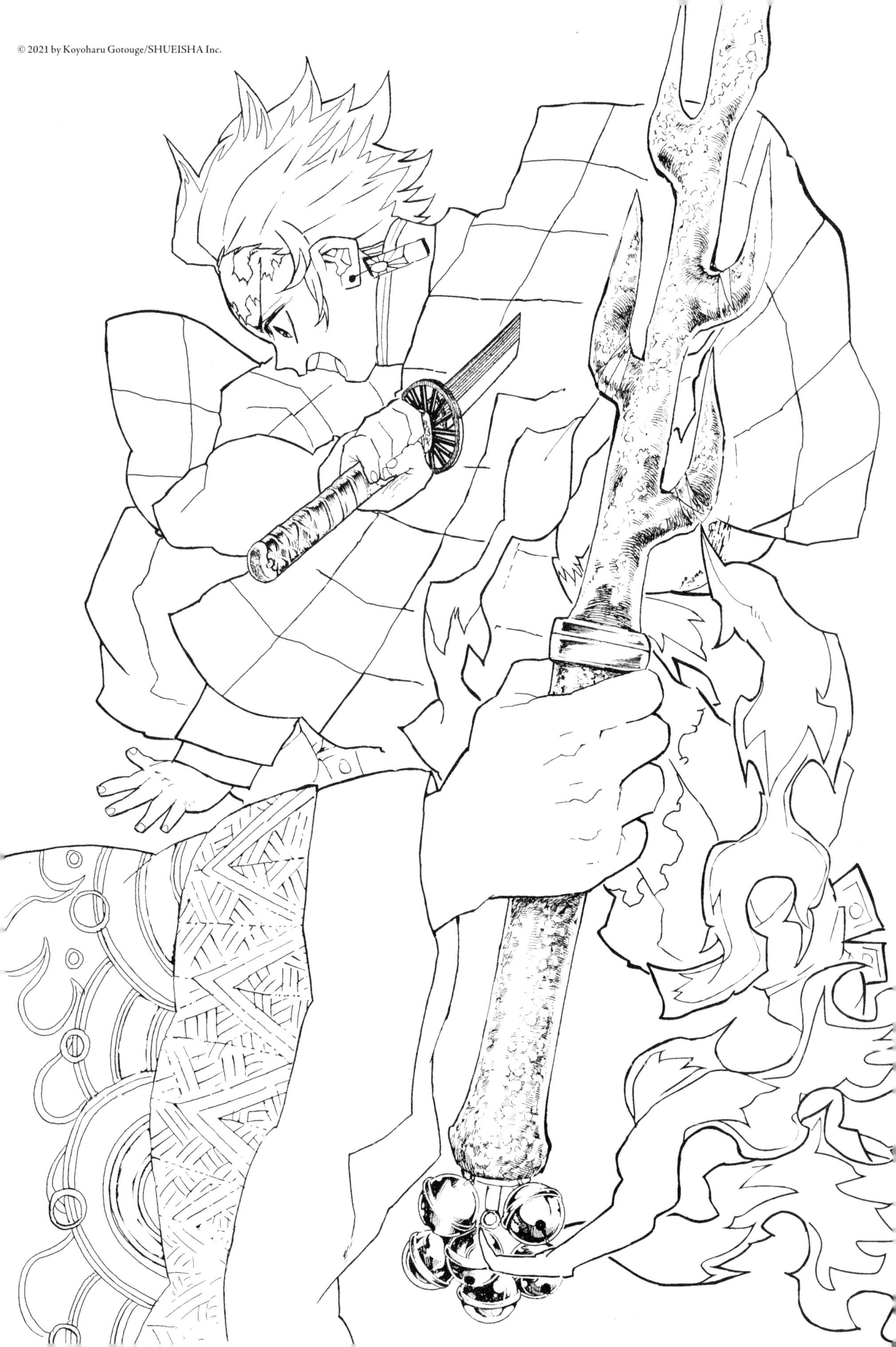

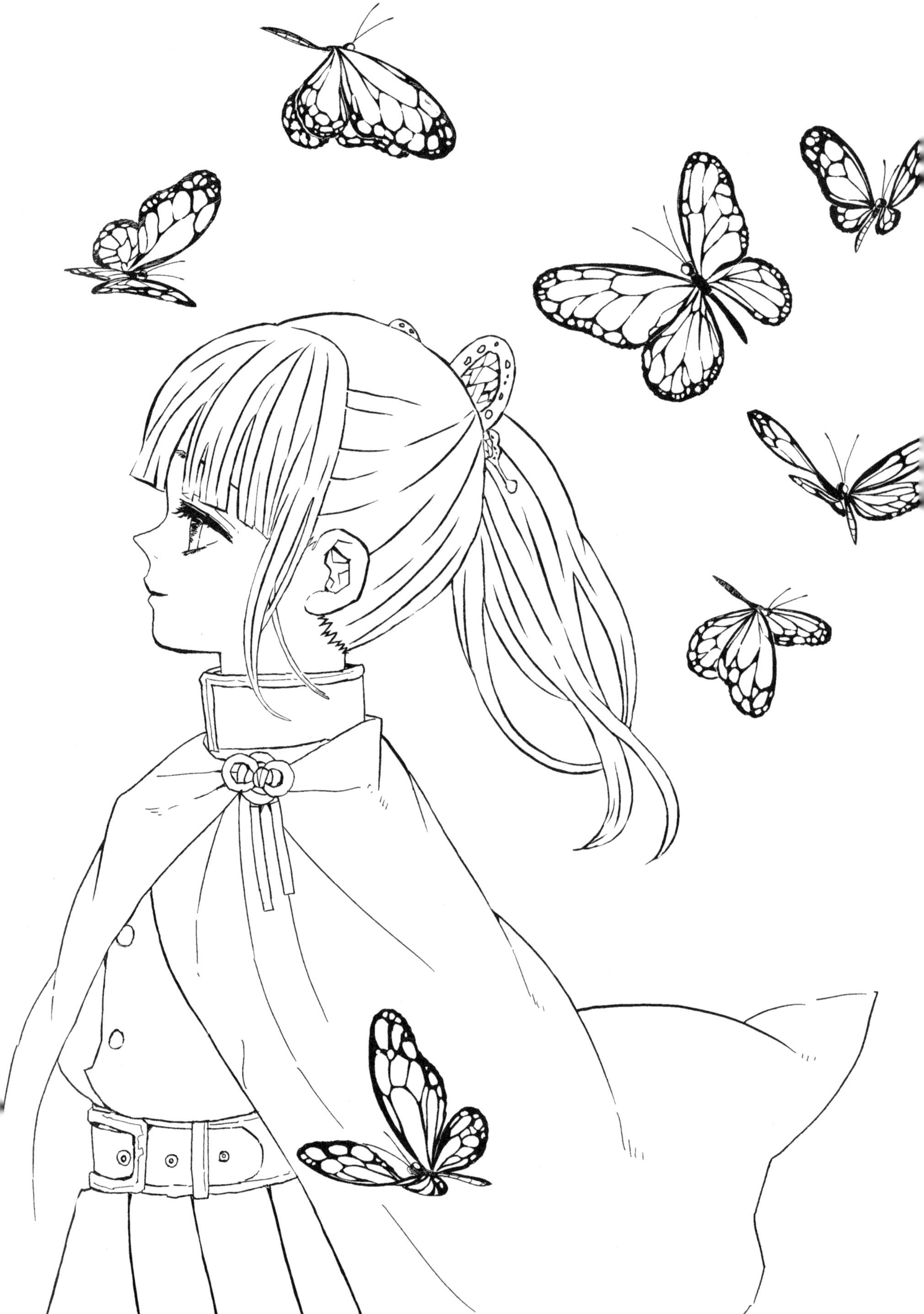

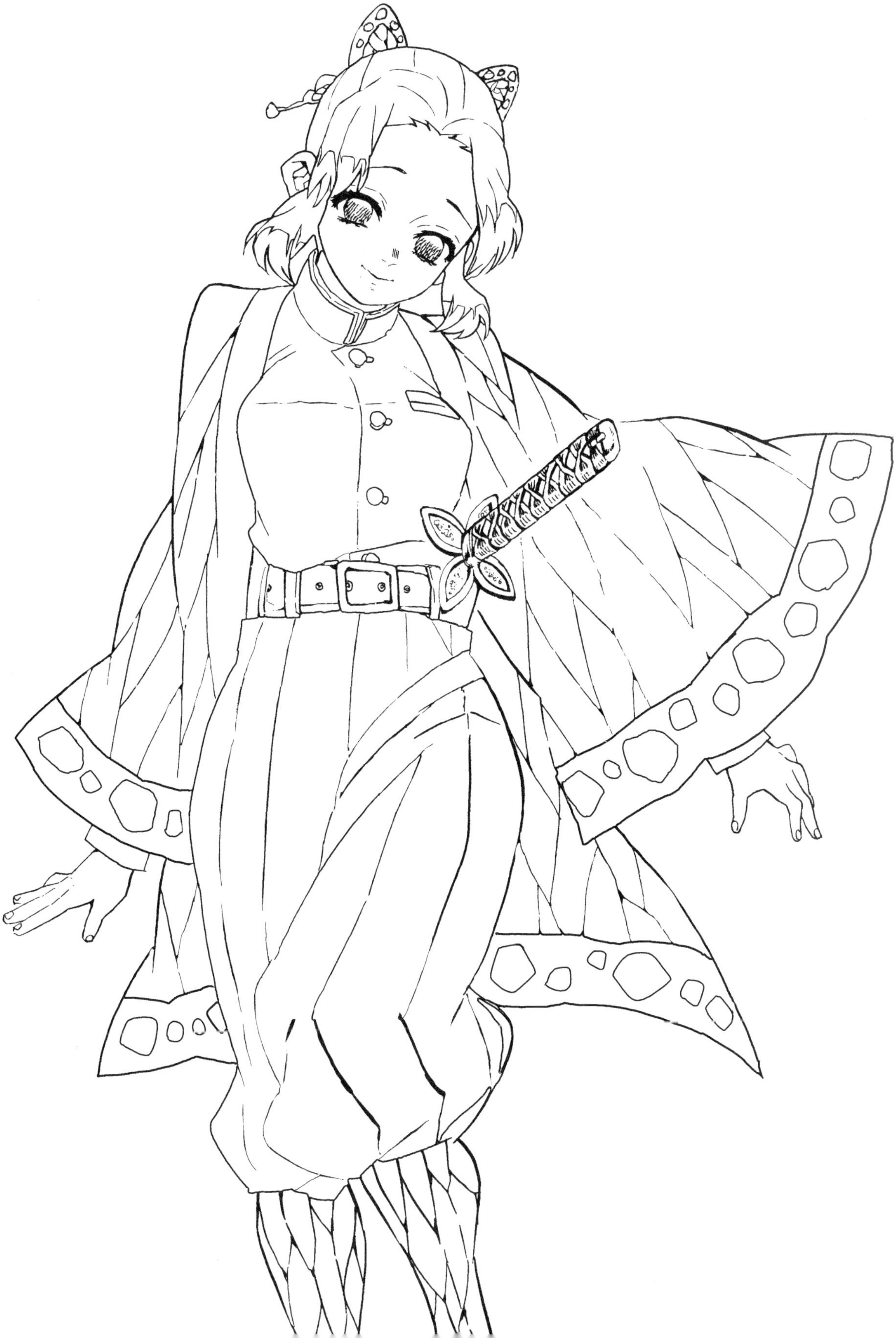

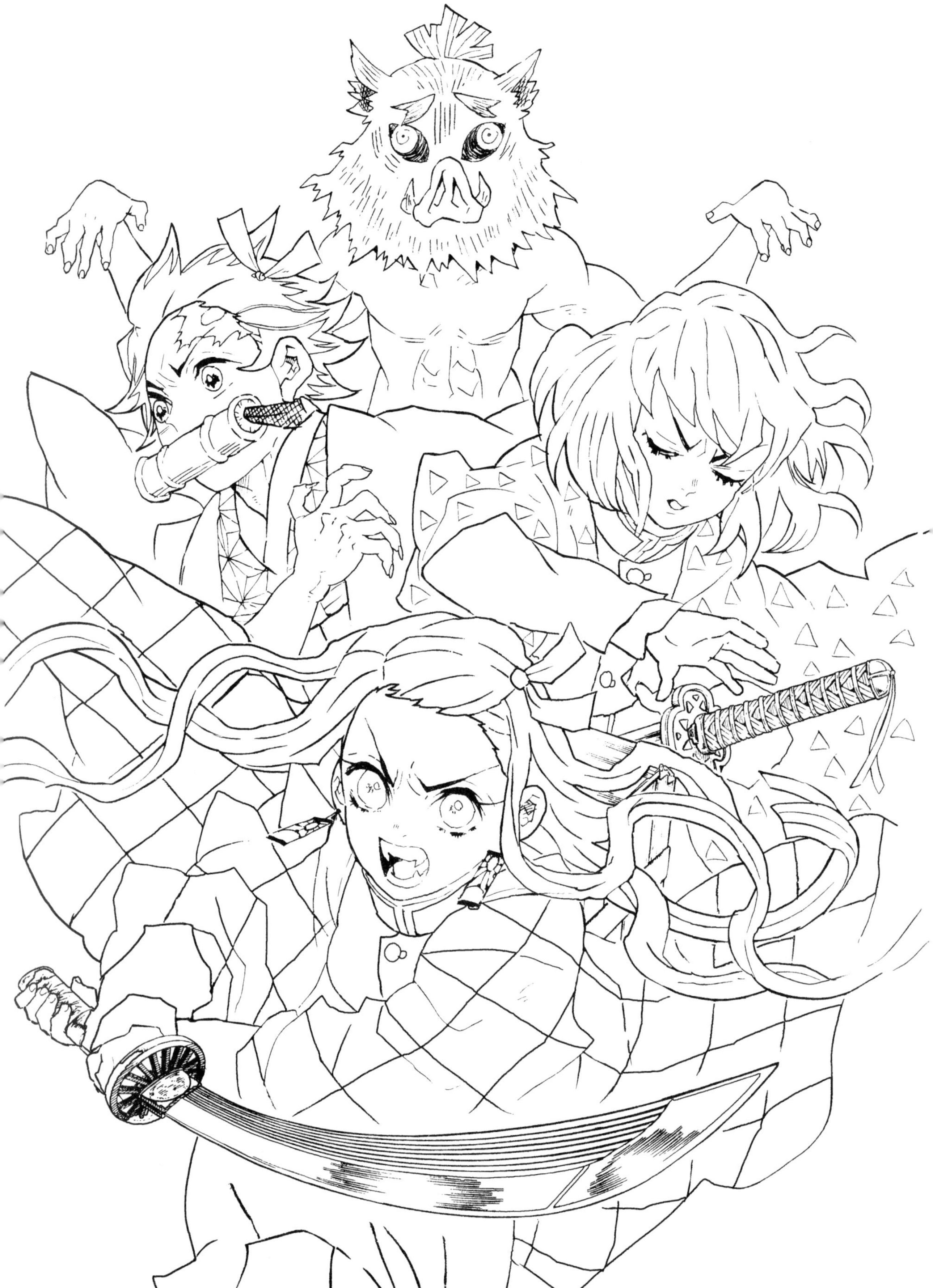

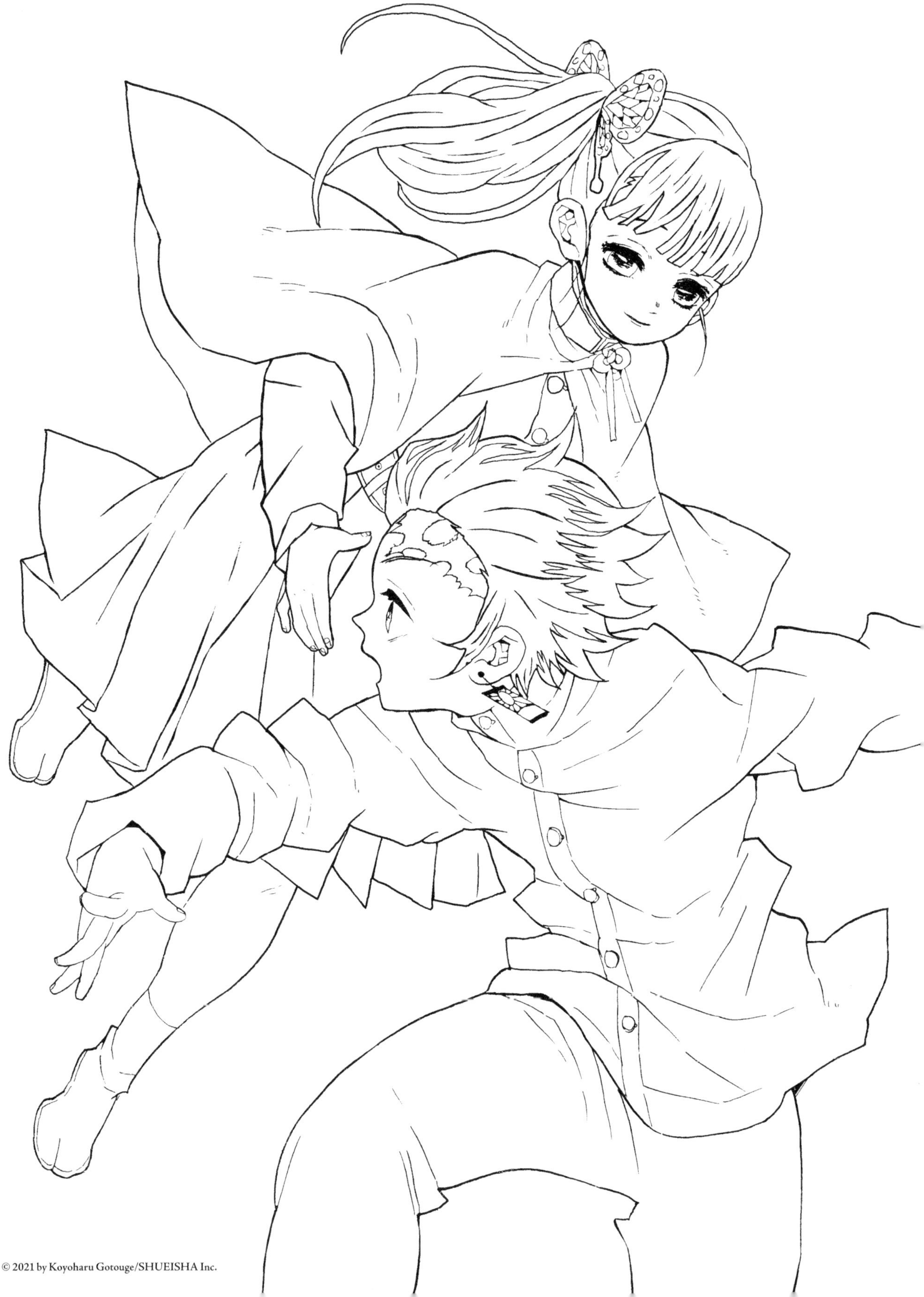

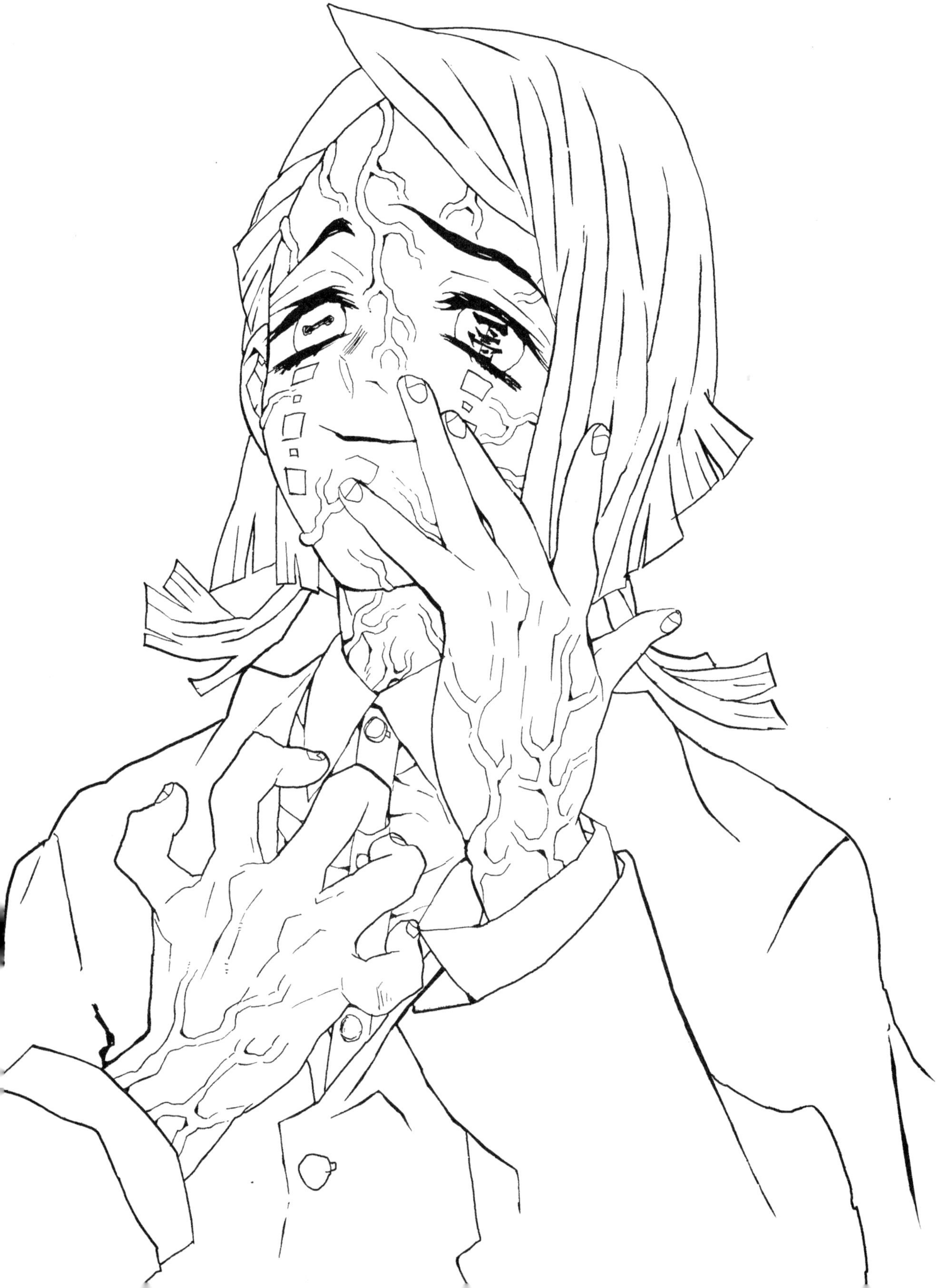

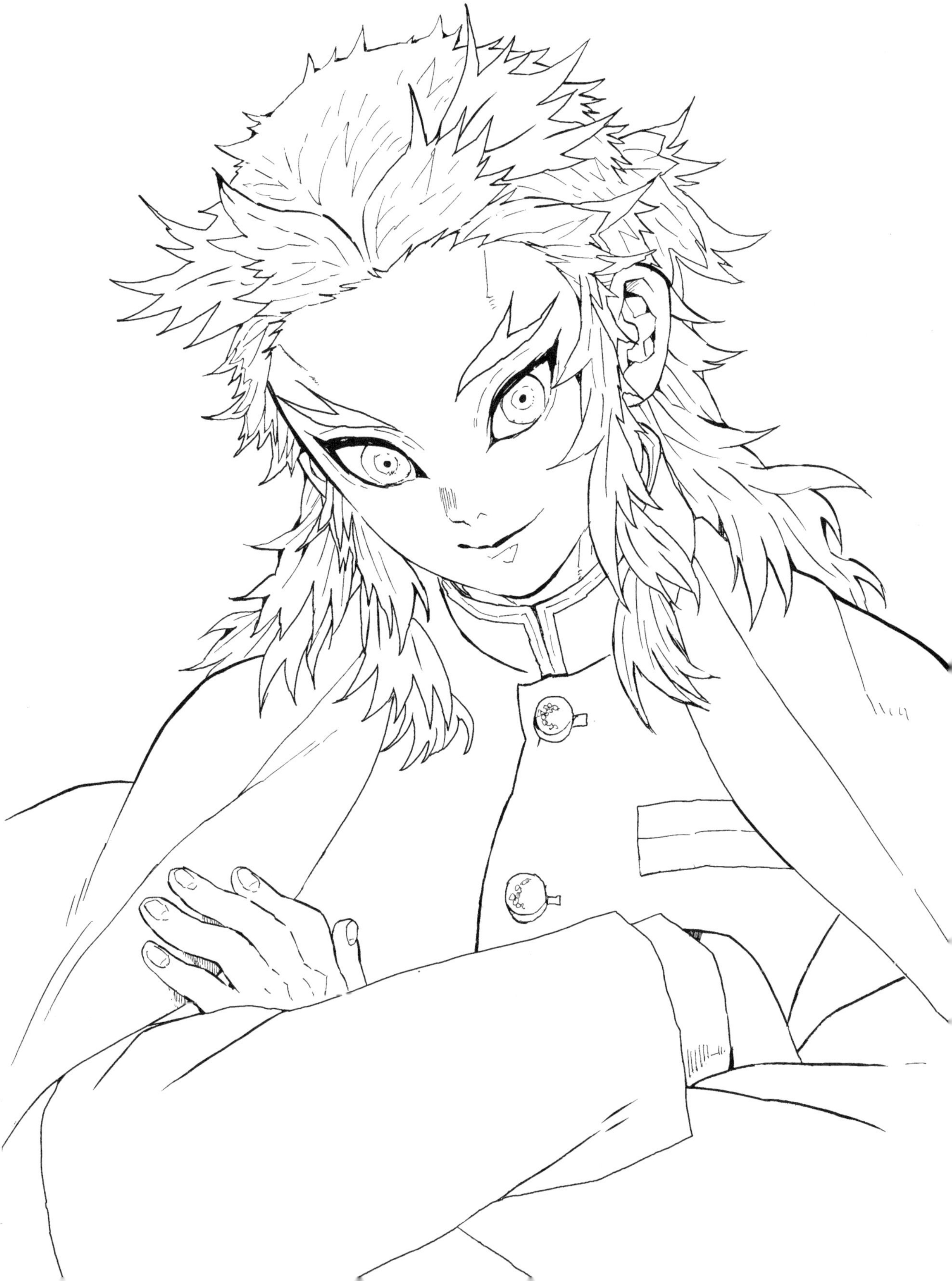

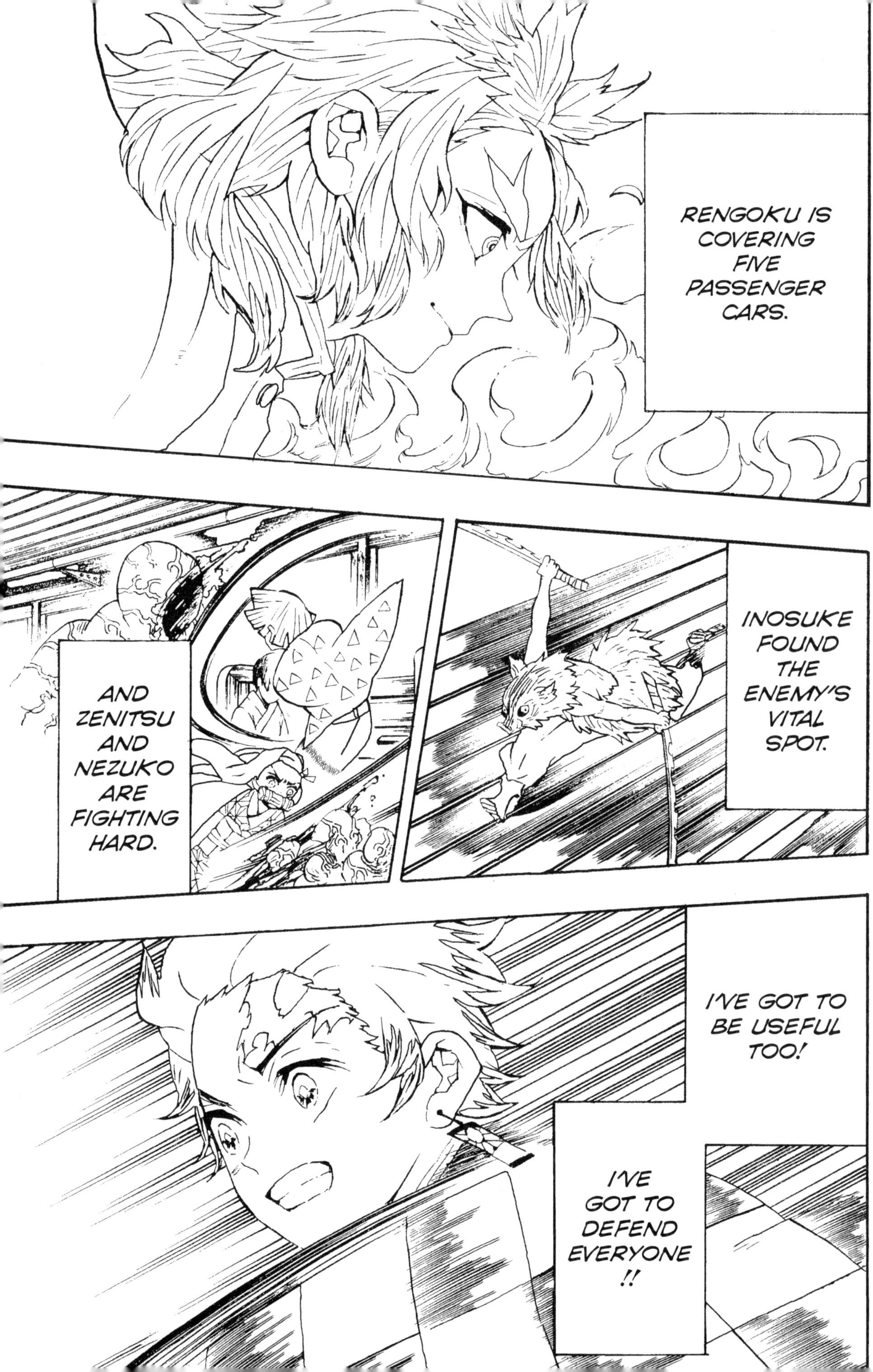
RENGOKU IS COVERING FIVE PASSENGER CARS.
INOSUKE FOUND THE ENEMY'S VITAL SPOT.
AND ZENITSU AND NEZUKO ARE FIGHTING HARD.
I'VE GOT TO BE USEFUL TOO!
I'VE GOT TO DEFEND EVERYONE!!

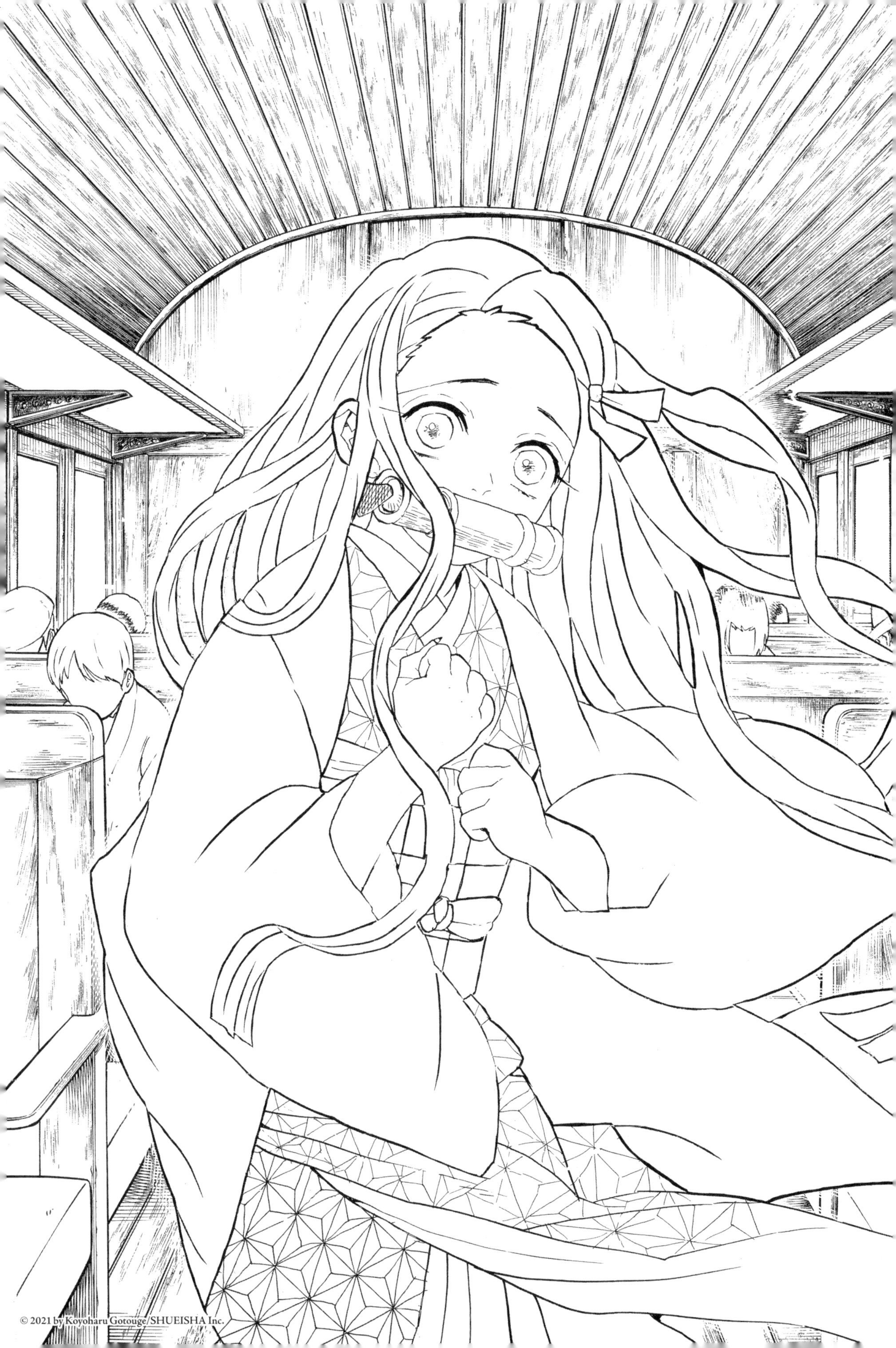

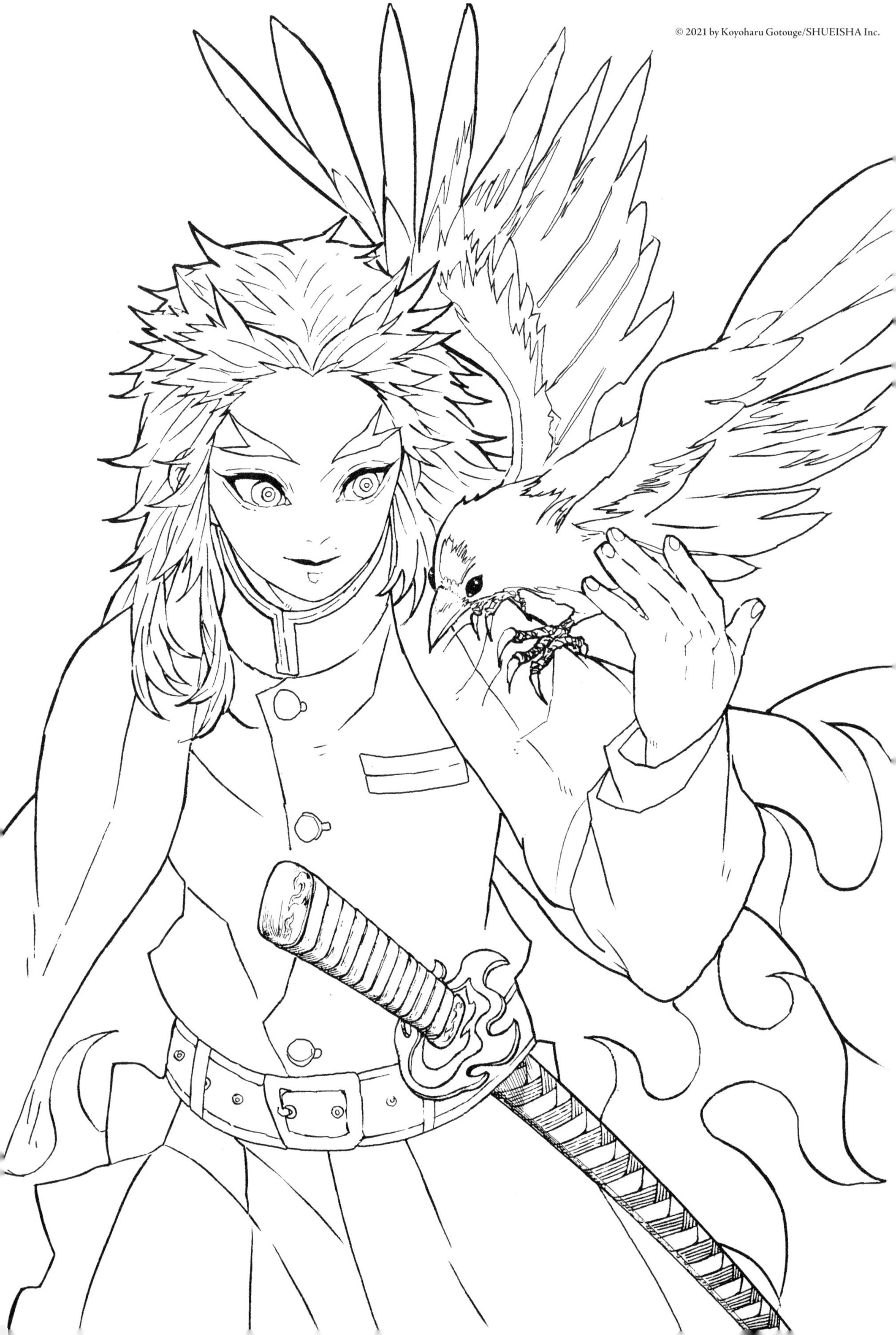

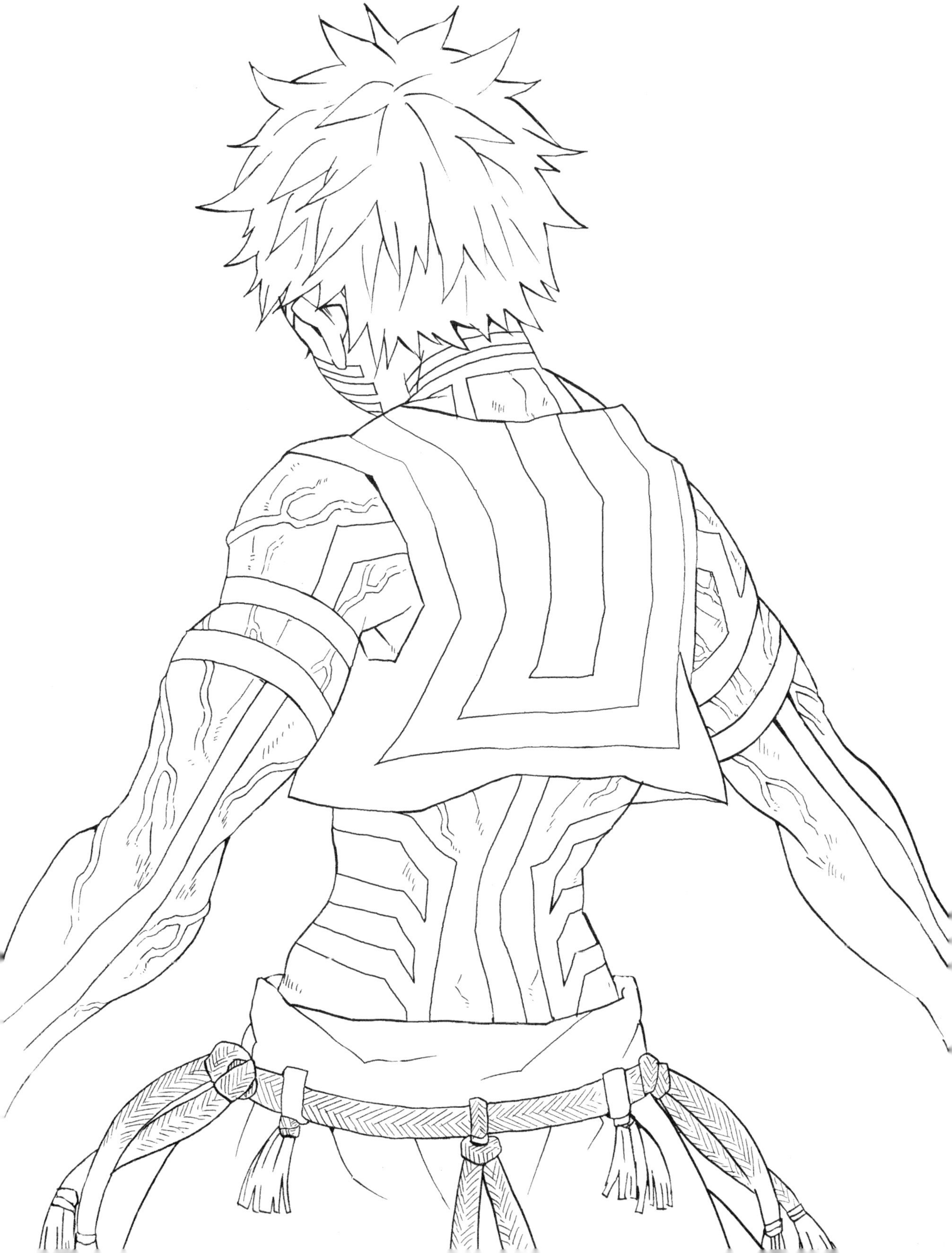

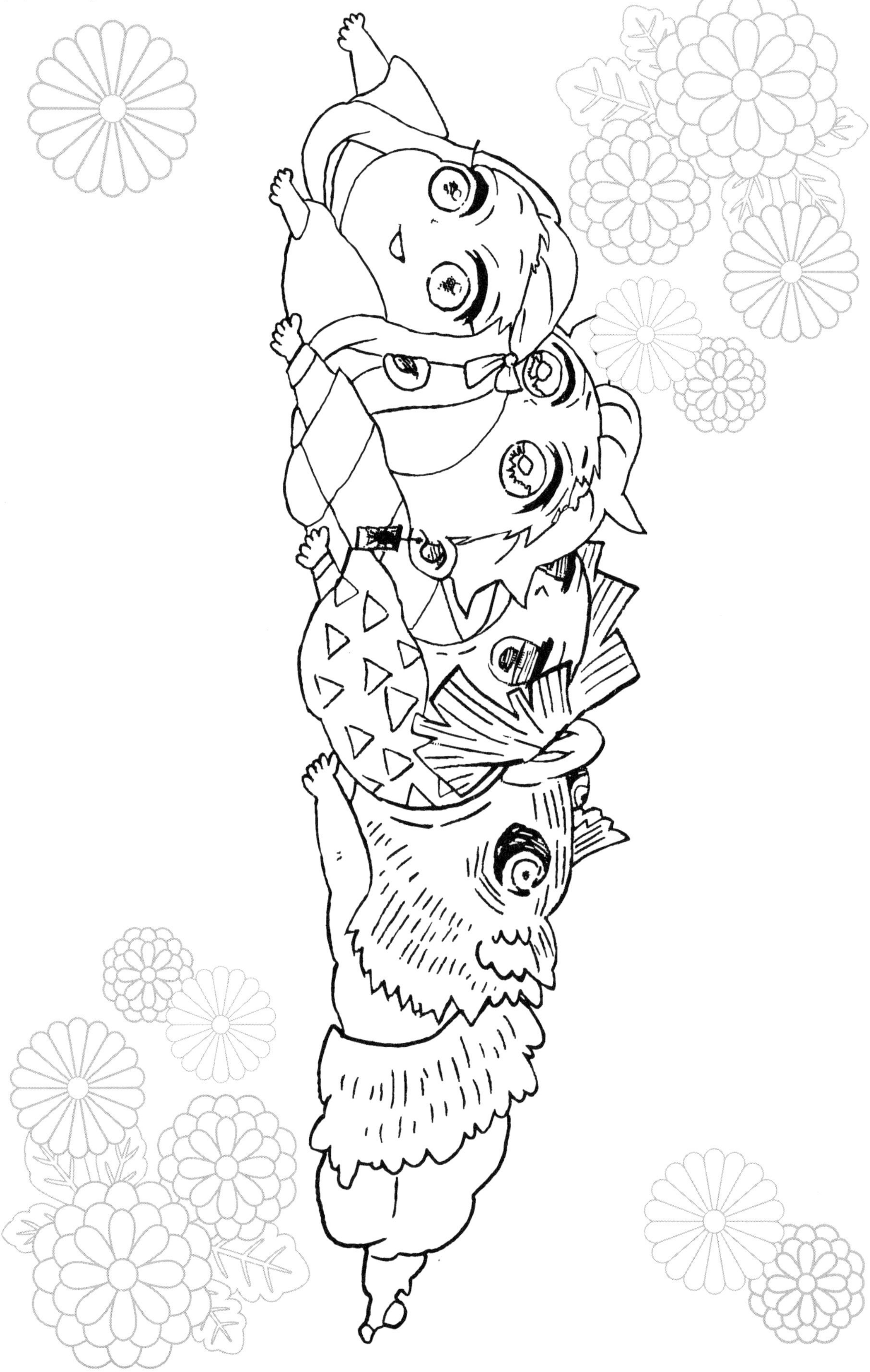

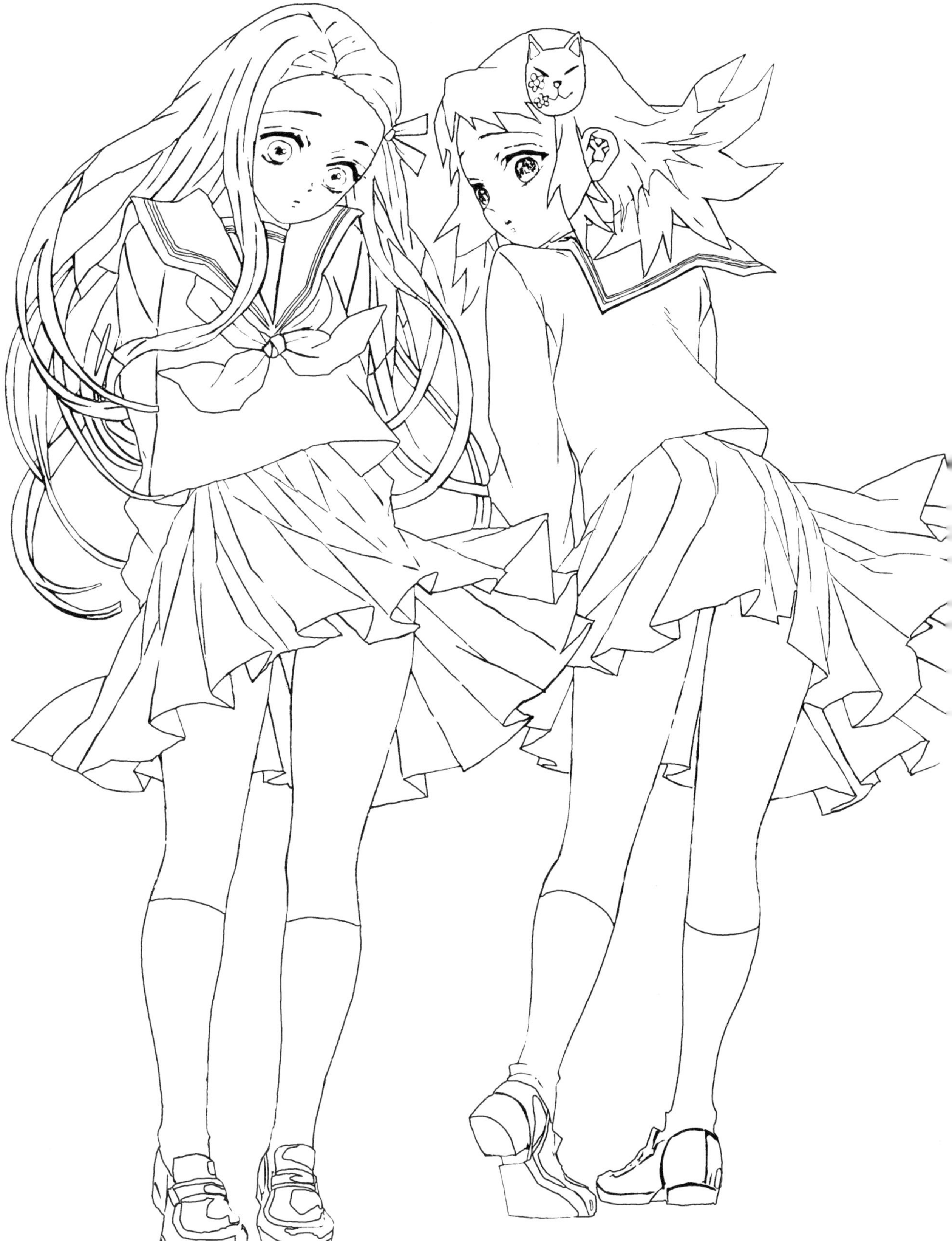

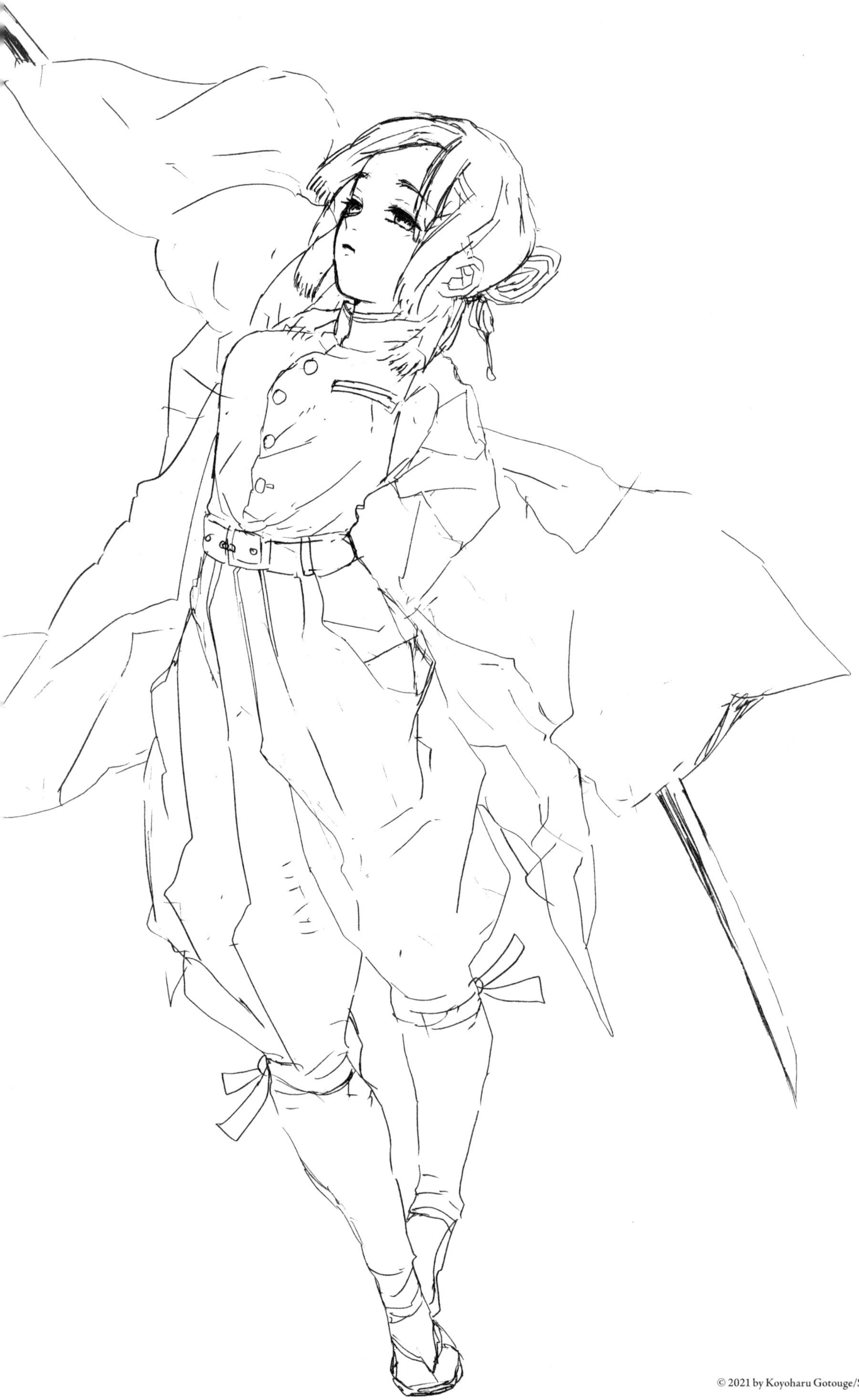

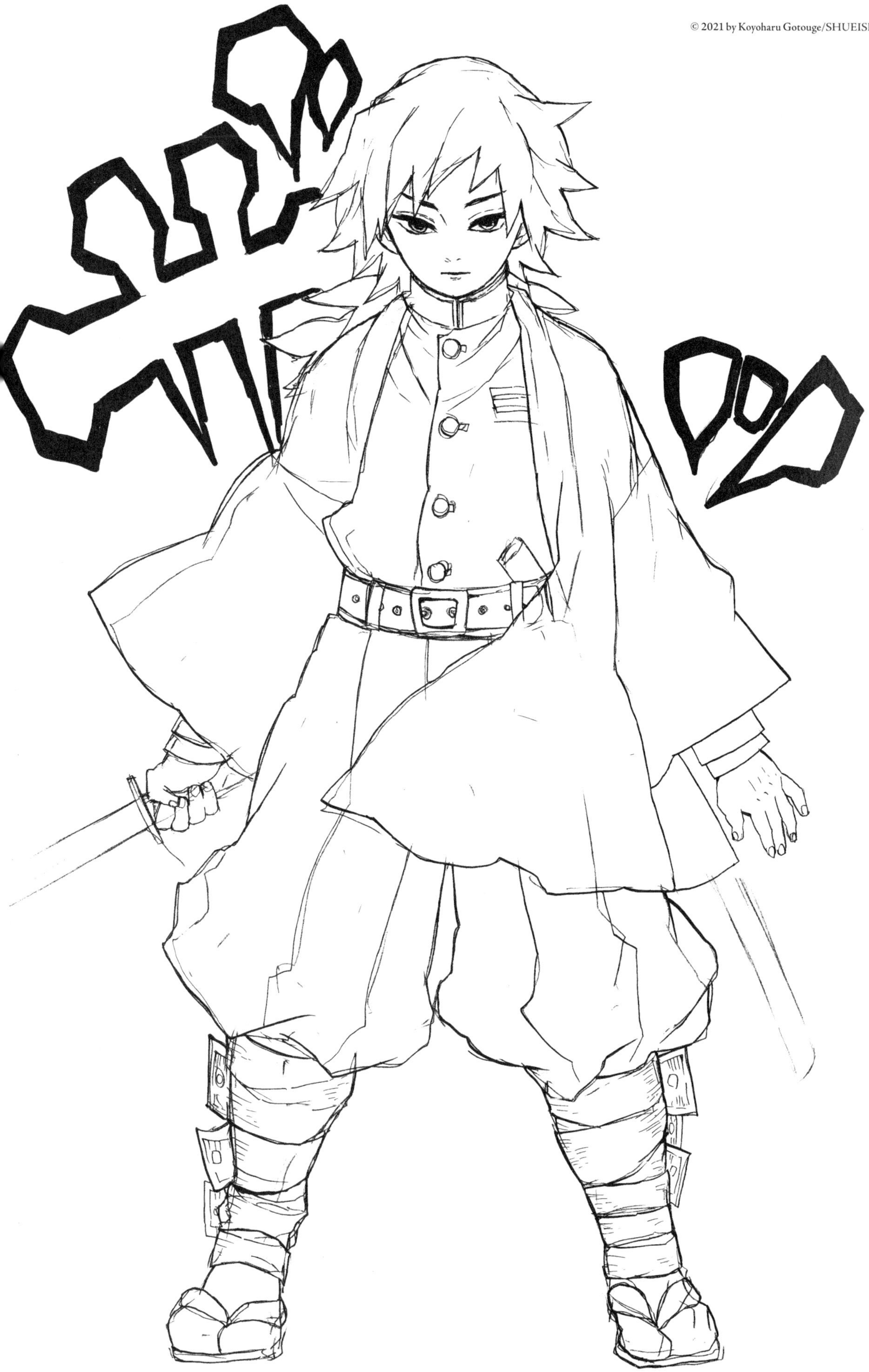

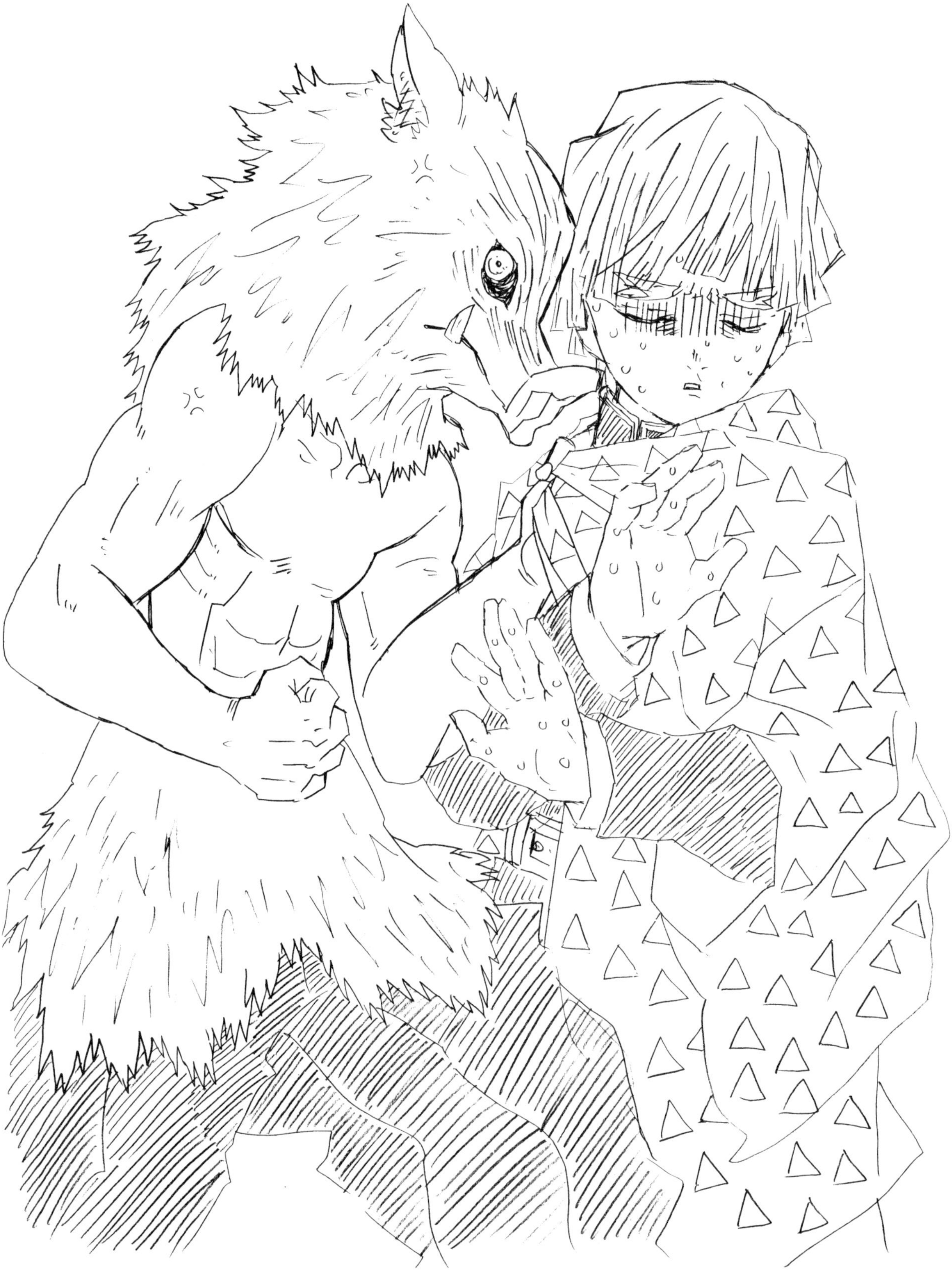

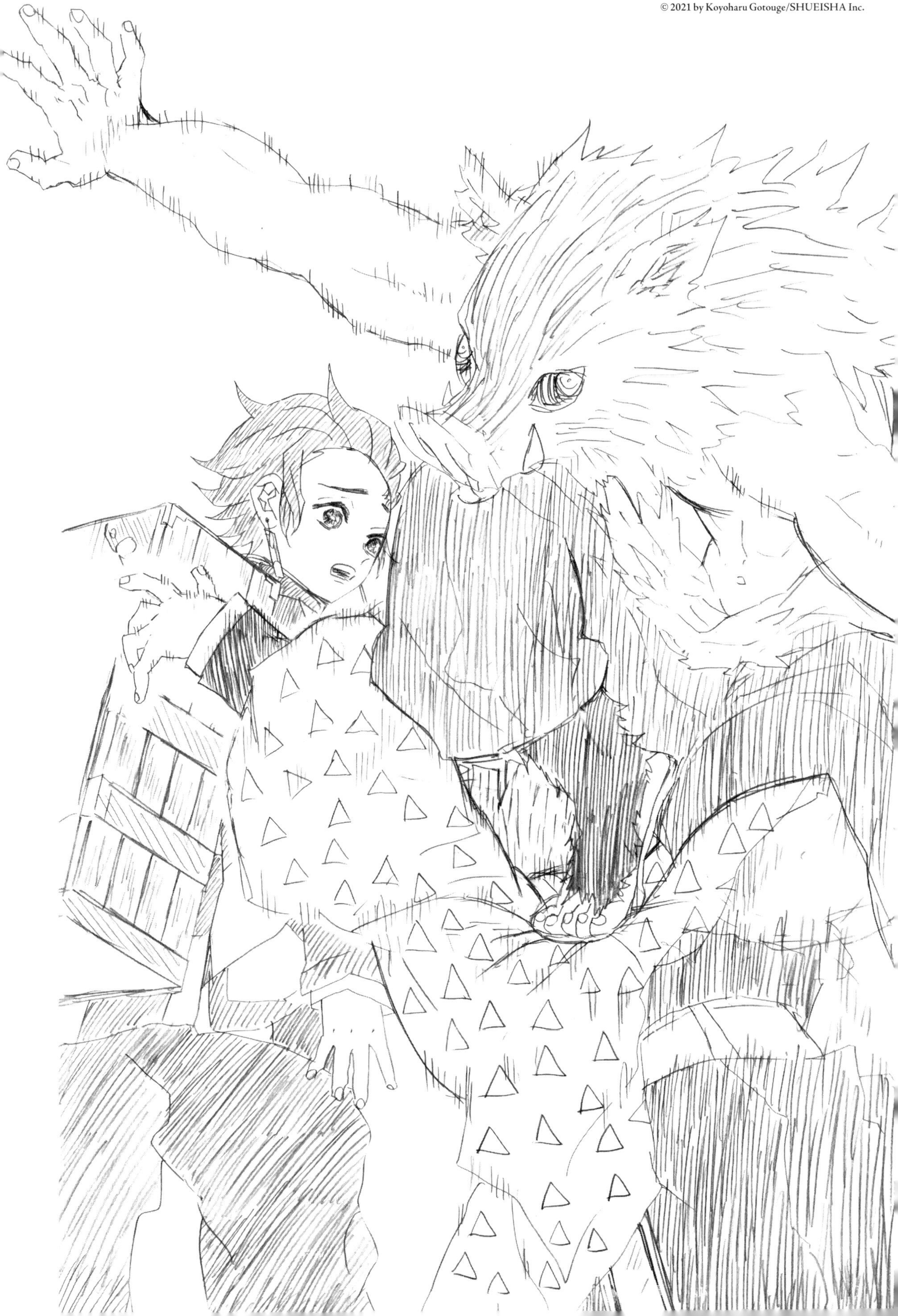

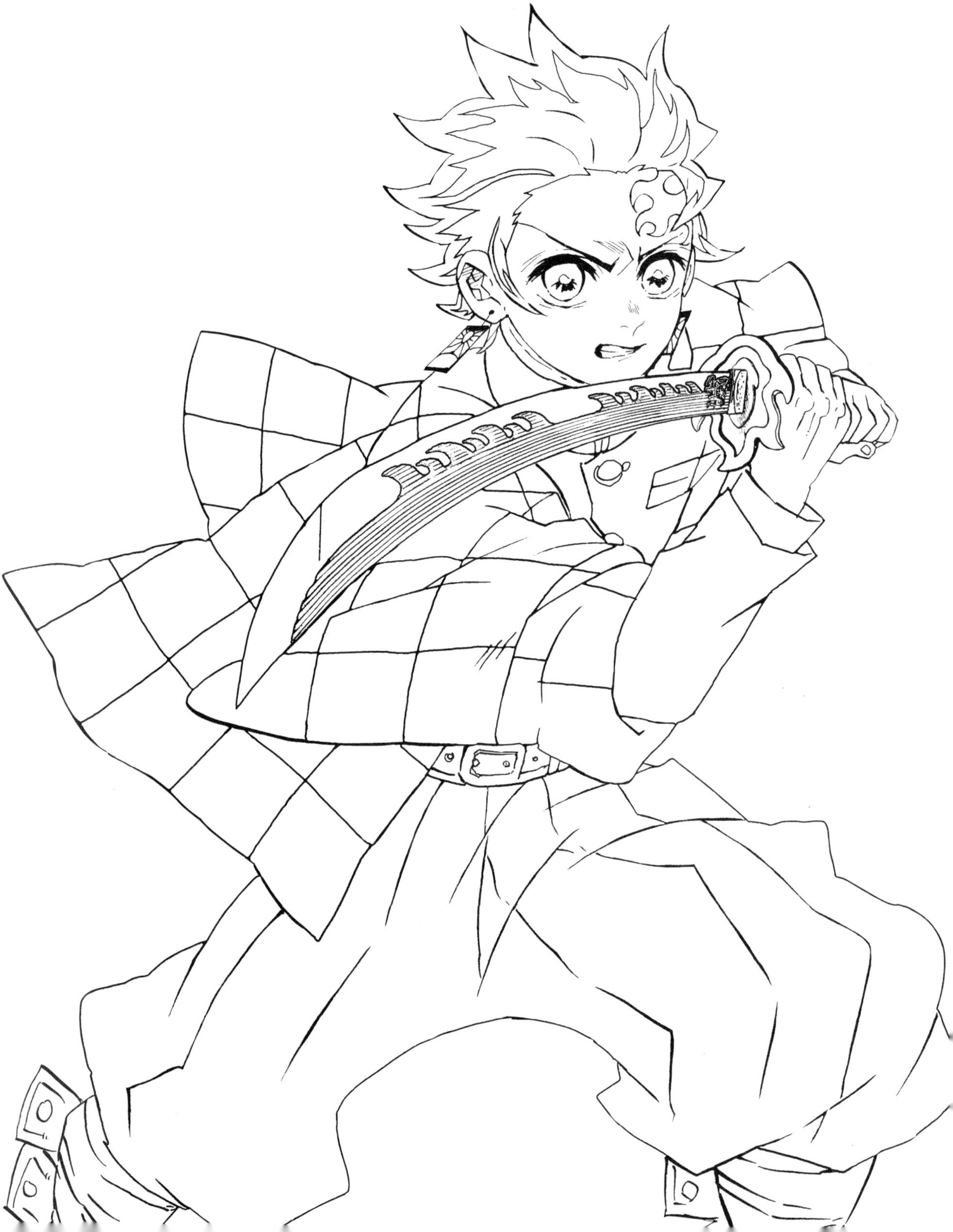

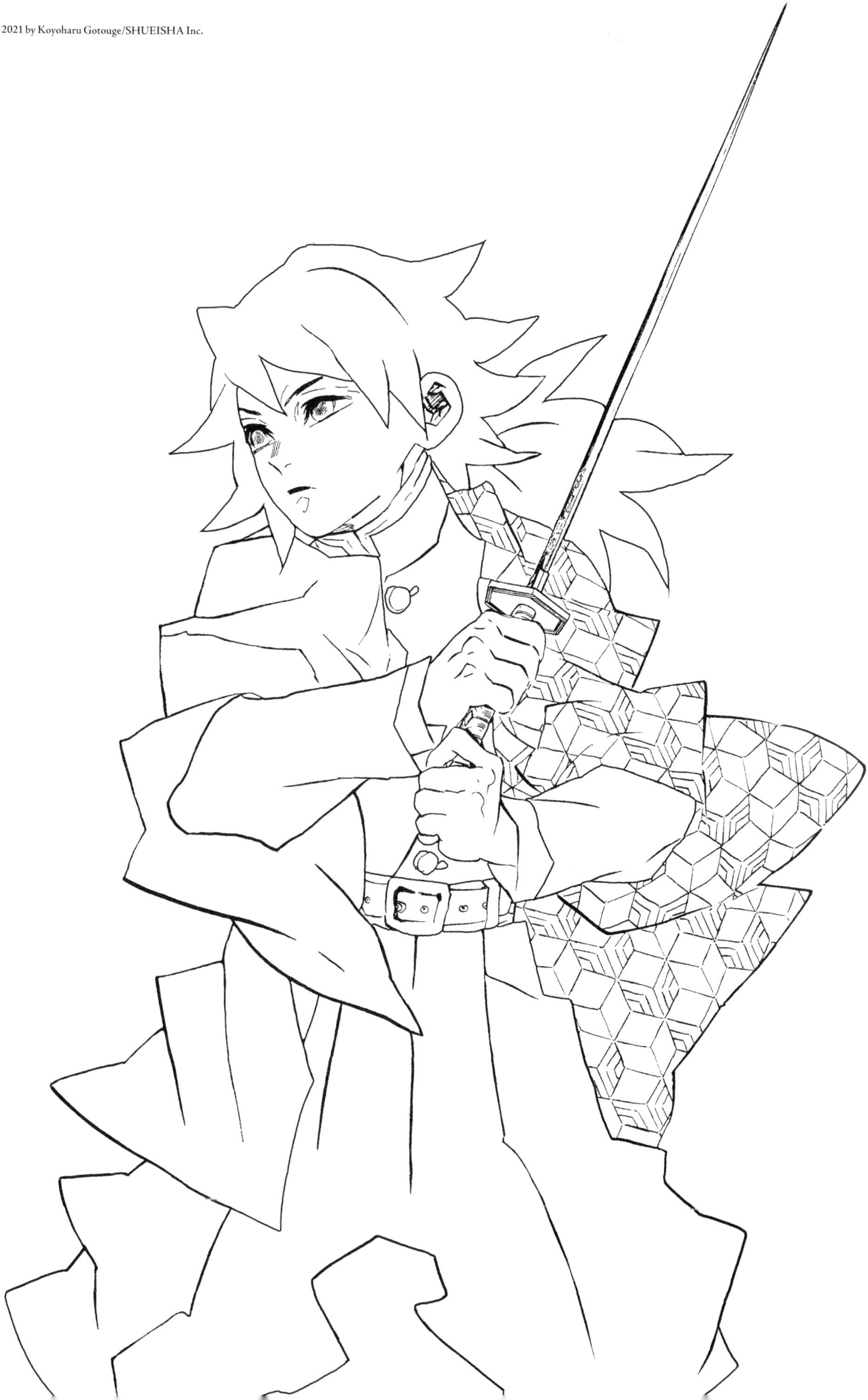

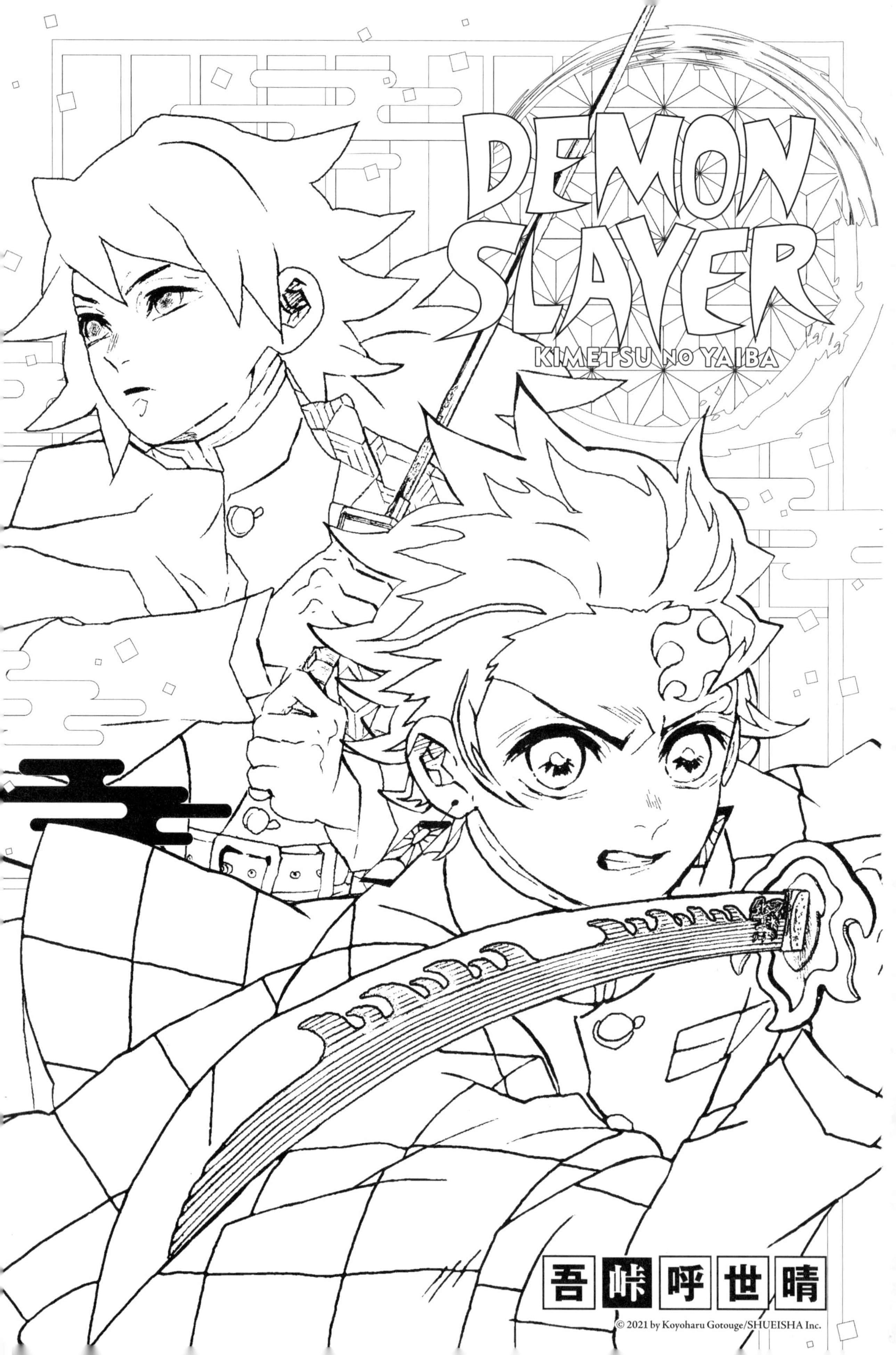
DEMON SLAYER
KIMETSU NO YAIBA
吾峠呼世晴
© 2021 by Koyoharu Gotouge/SHUEISHA Inc.